MASS MEDIA

OPPOSING VIEWPOINTS®

Other Books of Related Interest

Opposing Viewpoints Series

American Values
Censorship
Child Welfare
Civil Liberties
Culture Wars
The Information Revolution
Media Violence
Pornography

Current Controversies Series

Computers and Society
Free Speech
The Information Highway
Violence in the Media

At Issue Series

The Future of the Internet
The Media and Politics

MASS MEDIA

OPPOSING VIEWPOINTS®

Byron L. Stay, Professor of Rhetoric and Communications
and Associate Dean at Mount St. Mary's College,
Emmitsburg, Maryland, Book Editor

David L. Bender, Publisher
Bruno Leone, Executive Editor
Bonnie Szumski, Editorial Director
David M. Haugen, Managing Editor

OPPOSING
VIEWPOINTS®
SERIES

Greenhaven Press, Inc., San Diego, California

Cover photo: PhotoDisc

Library of Congress Cataloging-in-Publication Data

Mass media : opposing viewpoints / Byron L. Stay, book ed.
    p.   cm. — (Opposing viewpoints series)
    Includes bibliographical references and index.
    ISBN 0-7377-0055-6 (lib. bdg. : alk. paper). —
ISBN 0-7377-0054-8 (pbk. : alk. paper)
    1. Mass media. I. Stay, Byron L., 1947–   . II. Series: Opposing
viewpoints series (Unnumbered)
P90 .M2926 1999
302.23—dc21   98-47722
                                                            CIP

Greenhaven Press, Inc., P.O. Box 289009
San Diego, CA 92198-9009

"Congress shall make no law...abridging the freedom of speech, or of the press."

First Amendment to the U.S. Constitution

The basic foundation of our democracy is the First Amendment guarantee of freedom of expression. The Opposing Viewpoints Series is dedicated to the concept of this basic freedom and the idea that it is more important to practice it than to enshrine it.

CONTENTS

WHY CONSIDER
OPPOSING VIEWPOINTS?

"The only way in which a human being can make some
  approach to knowing the whole of a subject is by hearing
  what can be said about it by persons of every variety of
  opinion and studying all modes in which it can be looked
  at by every character of mind. No wise man ever acquired
  his wisdom in any mode but this."

John Stuart Mill

In our media-intensive culture it is not difficult to find differing
opinions. Thousands of newspapers and magazines and dozens
of radio and television talk shows resound with differing points
of view. The difficulty lies in deciding which opinion to agree
with and which "experts" seem the most credible. The more in-
undated we become with differing opinions and claims, the
more essential it is to hone critical reading and thinking skills to
evaluate these ideas. Opposing Viewpoints books address this
problem directly by presenting stimulating debates that can be
used to enhance and teach these skills. The varied opinions contained in each book examine many different aspects of a single
issue. While examining these conveniently edited opposing
views, readers can develop critical thinking skills such as the
ability to compare and contrast authors' credibility, facts, argu-
mentation styles, use of persuasive techniques, and other stylis-
tic tools. In short, the Opposing Viewpoints Series is an ideal
way to attain the higher-level thinking and reading skills so essential in a culture of diverse and contradictory opinions.

In addition to providing a tool for critical thinking, Opposing
Viewpoints books challenge readers to question their own
strongly held opinions and assumptions. Most people form their
opinions on the basis of upbringing, peer pressure, and personal, cultural, or professional bias. By reading carefully bal-
anced opposing views, readers must directly confront new ideas
as well as the opinions of those with whom they disagree. This
is not to simplistically argue that everyone who reads opposing
views will—or should—change his or her opinion. Instead, the
series enhances readers' understanding of their own views by
encouraging confrontation with opposing ideas. Careful examination of others' views can lead to the readers' understanding of
the logical inconsistencies in their own opinions, perspective on

why they hold an opinion, and the consideration of the possibility that their opinion requires further evaluation.

EVALUATING OTHER OPINIONS

To ensure that this type of examination occurs, Opposing Viewpoints books present all types of opinions. Prominent spokespeople on different sides of each issue as well as well-known professionals from many disciplines challenge the reader. An additional goal of the series is to provide a forum for other, less known, or even unpopular viewpoints. The opinion of an ordinary person who has had to make the decision to cut off life support from a terminally ill relative, for example, may be just as valuable and provide just as much insight as a medical ethicist's professional opinion. The editors have two additional purposes in including these less known views. One, the editors encourage readers to respect others' opinions—even when not enhanced by professional credibility. It is only by reading or listening to and objectively evaluating others' ideas that one can determine whether they are worthy of consideration. Two, the inclusion of such viewpoints encourages the important critical thinking skill of objectively evaluating an author's credentials and bias. This evaluation will illuminate an author's reasons for taking a particular stance on an issue and will aid in readers' evaluation of the author's ideas.

As series editors of the Opposing Viewpoints Series, it is our hope that these books will give readers a deeper understanding of the issues debated and an appreciation of the complexity of even seemingly simple issues when good and honest people disagree. This awareness is particularly important in a democratic society such as ours in which people enter into public debate to determine the common good. Those with whom one disagrees should not be regarded as enemies but rather as people whose views deserve careful examination and may shed light on one's own.

Thomas Jefferson once said that "difference of opinion leads to inquiry, and inquiry to truth." Jefferson, a broadly educated man, argued that "if a nation expects to be ignorant and free . . . it expects what never was and never will be." As individuals and as a nation, it is imperative that we consider the opinions of others and examine them with skill and discernment. The Opposing Viewpoints Series is intended to help readers achieve this goal.

David L. Bender & Bruno Leone,
Series Editors

Greenhaven Press anthologies primarily consist of previously published material taken from a variety of sources, including periodicals, books, scholarly journals, newspapers, government documents, and position papers from private and public organizations. These original sources are often edited for length and to ensure their accessibility for a young adult audience. The anthology editors also change the original titles of these works in order to clearly present the main thesis of each viewpoint and to explicitly indicate the opinion presented in the viewpoint. These alterations are made in consideration of both the reading and comprehension levels of a young adult audience. Every effort is made to ensure that Greenhaven Press accurately reflects the original intent of the authors included in this anthology.

INTRODUCTION

"Asking North Americans about the pervasive influence of media in this culture is a bit like . . . asking fish about water. 'Water? What water?' We live and breathe media—but we are largely unaware of how they shape our lives."
—Tom Montgomery-Fate, The Other Side, March/April 1997.

Few twentieth-century institutions have influenced Americans as much as the mass media. Especially since World War II, television, radio, and more recently the Internet have encroached into the lives of people from all classes and walks of life. The media generate an increasing wealth of information and services daily. In their purest form, the media provide the populace with the information it needs to function as a democracy. Matthew P. McAllister, in his book *The Commercialization of American Culture*, observes that "a well-developed media system, informing and teaching its citizens, helps democracy move toward its ideal state."

In addition to informing the populace, this boundless store of information provokes controversy. Many people object to the quality of much of the material found in the media—especially violent and sexually explicit material. These critics respond by supporting legislation that places limits on media content. Some laws forbid the production and distribution of material deemed obscene or indecent. Others mandate the use of technological devices that restrict programming that is considered inappropriate. However, such attempts to regulate the media are not welcomed by everyone. Many people are adamantly opposed to placing restrictions on media content, claiming that these restrictions violate the right to free speech.

Freedom of speech has become an indelible part of Western culture. Its origins can be traced as far back as sixteenth-century Britain, and it became a central tenet in the Declaration of the Rights of Man and of the Citizen, which came out of the French Revolution in 1789. In the United States it is unlikely that the Constitution would have been ratified if it did not contain the first ten amendments, known as the Bill of Rights. The First Amendment says that "Congress shall make no law . . . abridging the freedom of speech, or of the press." Originally, the "press" meant primarily newspapers, books, magazines, and eventually motion pictures, but the term has since come to refer to radio, television, and the Internet as well.

Freedom of the press is not absolute, however. The First Amendment also provides that no works can be published that "present a clear and present danger that they will bring about the substantive evils that Congress [or the state] has a right to prevent." In the modern age there are numerous problems with determining what speech is harmful and with deciding how the harm can be effectively reduced without unnecessarily restricting free speech. The tension between the public's right to free speech and the government's right to regulate harmful speech is thus a central issue in debates over the mass media. Two current topics in which this tension is particularly pronounced are the debate over pornography on the Internet and violence on television.

The Internet is a particularly difficult technology to monitor because, unlike radio, television, and newspapers, the information is not generated from a limited number of outlets, but from a galaxy of websites and research engines. As a result, it has become nearly impossible to monitor Internet information from the point of origin. Anyone can access sites, including pornographic ones, easily and privately. Those who wish to restrict pornographic Internet sites either support technological methods, like Internet filtering software, or legislation requiring service providers to monitor and limit pornography. Walter S. Baer, a communications and information policy specialist at RAND, writes that "government laws and regulations should encourage technical and other means to enable us to determine what kinds of information we let into our homes." Many people, like Baer, believe that technological solutions are better than legislative ones because they preserve the freedom of the media while protecting children from exposure to inappropriate material.

Others believe that both of these methods of restricting Internet content have serious flaws. They contend that no effective way to screen out pornography on the Internet has been developed. In some cases the pornography is not clearly labeled and is immune to blocking systems. In other cases the pornography is successfully blocked along with other nonpornographic sites. In September 1998, when Congress released the text of Kenneth Starr's report on President Bill Clinton on the Internet, many of the details were so graphic that some congressmen wondered publicly whether or not it should have been edited or summarized instead. Filtering devices designed to identify pornographic sites through keywords or through subject matter may well have identified the report as pornographic.

An issue closely related to Internet pornography is whether violence on television presents a danger to children and, if so, what can be done about it. Many commentators insist that children who view violence on television are more likely to engage in aggressive behavior. Therefore, they argue, violent media programming should not be protected by the First Amendment. Kevin W. Saunders, in his book *Violence as Obscenity*, argues that there should be no distinction between obscenity and violence. "There are no theories of the First Amendment," he writes, "that justify an exception for sexual obscenity that cannot be reasonably extended to justify an exception for what might be described as violent obscenity."

Other researchers question whether television violence does in fact cause violence. Jonathan L. Freedman, a professor of psychology at the University of Toronto, argues that although children imitate what they see on television, the link between such imitation and societal violence is not clear. After all, television villains usually start the violence and are punished for it. A child may learn how to execute a karate kick on television, according to Freedman, but that does not mean that television has caused the child to be an aggressive person. "Television is an easy target for the concern about violence in our society," he writes, "but a misleading one." Freedman and others who question the causal link between television violence and real-life violence object to efforts to regulate violent television programming.

Although considerable disagreement exists between those who promote unfettered access to the media and those who believe that the media must be restricted, there is no question that the mass media are among the most pervasive elements of modern culture. The media will continue to exert a strong influence on politics and pocketbooks, on recreation and on the marketplace. These are the issues explored in *Mass Media: Opposing Viewpoints*, which contains the following chapters: How Does Television Affect Society? Is Advertising Harmful to Society? How Do the Media Influence Politics? Should Pornography on the Internet Be Regulated? Are Television Content Regulations Beneficial for Children? The varying opinions expressed here reveal and explore the important place the mass media occupy in American society and culture.

CHAPTER 1

HOW DOES TELEVISION AFFECT SOCIETY?

Chapter Preface

Nearly forty years after Federal Communications Commission chairman Newton Minow referred to television as a "vast wasteland," the effect of television's influence on society continues to be of great concern. Many people believe that television has a corrosive effect on the nation's moral fabric and contributes to social problems—especially violence. For example, the American Psychological Association reports that American children witness 8,000 murders and 100,000 violent acts on television before they graduate from elementary school. Numerous studies have been done in an attempt to confirm that viewing television violence leads to violent behavior among children as well as adults. According to psychologist Madeline Levine, more than 1,000 studies have been conducted on the link between media violence and societal violence among children. Of these studies, 996 have confirmed "that media violence encourages aggression."

Other people reject the charge that television violence plays a significant role in causing real-life violence. Jonathan Freedman, a professor of psychology at the University of Toronto, sees major flaws in the studies that have claimed to establish a causal connection between television violence and aggressive behavior. After reviewing these studies, he concludes, "Television is an easy target for the concern about violence in our society but a misleading one. We should no longer waste time worrying about this subject. Instead let us turn our attention to the obvious major causes of violence, which include poverty, racial conflict, drug abuse, and poor parenting."

Television's impact on society—including its potential contribution to societal violence—is the topic of the following chapter.

| "The evidence seems strong that viewing violent television causes aggression."

TELEVISION VIOLENCE CAUSES SOCIETAL VIOLENCE

Kevin W. Saunders

In the following viewpoint, Kevin W. Saunders discusses four methods of researching the relationship between television violence and real-world violence: laboratory studies, field studies, correlational studies, and meta-analysis. Although he believes it is impossible to establish an absolute cause-and-effect link between media violence and violent behavior, he maintains that all four research methods provide strong evidence that such a link exists. Studies of the brains of rats have provided additional support to this claim, according to Saunders. Saunders is author of the 1996 book *Violence as Obscenity: Limiting the Media's First Amendment Protection*.

As you read, consider the following questions:

1. What does "meta-analysis" mean, as explained by Saunders?
2. Why does the author believe meta-analysis is a good way to study television violence?
3. According to the author, what is the difference between "causation" and "correlation"?

Excerpted from "The Social Science Debate on the Causative Effect of Media Violence," in *Violence as Obscenity: Limiting the Media's First Amendment Protection*, by Kevin W. Saunders. Copyright 1996, Duke University Press. Reprinted with permission. Endnotes in the original have been omitted in this reprint.

I t is clear that much of the social concern over media violence, and in particular television violence, is due to a belief that such depictions cause real violence. It is important to understand the variety of causation under consideration. Obviously, to claim that certain depictions cause violence is not to claim that every person exposed to such material commits acts of violence nor that only such people commit such acts. The issue is, instead, one of probability and correlation. The question is whether a population exposed to depictions of violence is more violent than a population without such exposure. There are several important studies and reports that attempt to answer that question.

In 1969, the National Commission on the Causes and Prevention of Violence issued a report claiming to have found a link between television violence and violent behavior in viewers. The staff report to the commission was clear in its conclusions that mass-media portrayal of violence has an effect on society. Among short-term effects, the report concluded that

> [e]xposure to mass medial portrayals of violence stimulates violent behavior when—(a) Subjects are either calm or anxious prior to exposure, but more so when they are frustrated, insulted, or otherwise angered. (b) Aggressive or violent cues are present (e.g., weapons of violence). (c) Subjects are exposed either to justified or unjustified violence, but more so when justified violence is portrayed.

The report also found the following statements on long-term effects to be consistent with the research findings and the most informed thinking in social science:

> Exposure to mass media portrayals of violence over a long period of time socializes audiences into the norms, attitudes, and values for violence contained in those portrayals . . . [as among other factors t]he primacy of the part played by violence in media presentations increases.

> Persons who have been effectively socialized by mass media portrayals of violence will, under a broad set of precipitating conditions, behave in accordance with the norms, attitudes, and values for violence contained in medial presentations. Persons who have been effectively socialized into the norms for violence in the television world of violence would behave in the following manner: . . . They would probably resolve conflict by the use of violence[,] use violence as a means to obtain desired ends[,] use a weapon when engaging in violence[, and i]f they were policemen, they would be likely to meet violence with violence, often escalating its level. . . .

Much of the early work on the effect of televised violence

consisted of experiments in the controlled environment of the laboratory. The work of Professor Albert Bandura and his associates has become the classic study. Bandura's study involved nursery school children who were individually exposed to aggressive behavior in various contexts. For one group, an adult was observed playing with various toys, including a five-foot inflatable Bobo doll. The adult model punched the doll, hit it in the head with a mallet, tossed it in the air, kicked it around the room, and sat on it, while punching it in the nose repeatedly. A second group was shown a film of an adult acting toward a Bobo doll in the same manner. A third group viewed similar action in a film designed to resemble a cartoon but actually involving a cartoon-like stage setting and a human actor costumed to look like a cartoon figure.

After observing the model or one of the films, each child was taken to another room containing attractive toys. The child was frustrated by being told that those toys were reserved for other children but that he or she could play with the toys in the next room. Those toys included nonaggressive toys, such as crayons and plastic farm animals, and aggressive toys, including a three-foot Bobo doll and a mallet. The children were observed playing with the toys and their total aggression levels were rated, with subratings for various forms of aggression. The levels of aggression demonstrated by all three groups were significantly higher than the level of aggression for a control group not exposed to the films or real-life model, and the aggression was elevated for both boys and girls. The scientists concluded that exposure to filmed aggression increases aggression, with those exposed to the films almost twice as aggressive as the control group. Further, they found no evidence that this learned aggression is limited to children who are naturally more aggressive than other children or who otherwise deviate from the behavioral norm. . . .

FIELD STUDIES

Field studies attempt to measure the relationship between television violence and aggressive behavior in experiments involving real-world settings. By examining the effects of television outside of the laboratory, the conclusions they draw are more exportable to the real world; they have greater external validity. On the other hand, since the controls that can be imposed in such settings are not as strong as in the laboratory, there is often room to question the internal validity of the results obtained. Furthermore, even the external validity is often affected by the fact that the settings employed may be somewhat artificial. The possibility of attack on two fronts has led to disagreement over what conclusions can be drawn from these studies.

As an example, Professor Jonathan Freedman, a skeptic on the point of television causing violence, and Professors Lynette Friedrich-Cofer and Aletha Huston, seemingly believers in such an effect, have both examined the same series of field experiments. In similar studies in the United States and Belgium, groups of boys, who were institutionalized because of delinquency or neglect, were shown either violent or nonviolent films for a one-week period. Friedrich-Cofer and Huston analyzed the results:

> In the Belgian study, physical aggression increased significantly . . . in both cottages assigned to violent films, but did not increase in the neutral film cottages. Total aggression, including both physical and verbal aggression, increased primarily in the violent film cottage that was initially more aggressive. In two U.S. studies total aggression was significantly higher in two cottages viewing television violence for 5 days than in cottages viewing neutral films. . . .

CORRELATIONAL STUDIES

Correlational studies do not manipulate variables to determine what effects may result. They are even more real-world in that they examine the demographics of populations in search of relations between demographic variables. The time period of the search may range from an analysis of data gathered at a particular time to an analysis of data gathered over an extended period. A second approach is to gather more detailed survey results from a particular population, again ranging from a single survey to a comparison of survey data gathered over a period of time. . . .

This second variety of correlational study is exemplified by the survey work of Doctors Monroe M. Lefkowitz, Leonard D. Eron, Leopold O. Walder, and L. Rowell Huesmann. Lefkowitz, et al., began their study in 1955 by examining all the children in the third grade in Columbia County, New York. They gathered data on each child from the child's parents and classmates and the child himself or herself. Each child was given an aggressiveness rating based on classmate response as to which children are most likely to disobey the teacher, start fights, push or shove others, take things from other children, etc. Interviews with parents were used to gather data for each child as to television viewing habits. Programs watched were rated for their violent content, and each child received a score based on his or her viewing of violence. The parent interviews also provided data on some forty other variables regarding personality, intelligence, social status and family situation, factors which had to be controlled for in the study. Follow-up surveys were conducted when the third graders reached the eighth grade and again after graduation from high school. Of 875 children in the initial sample, 460 responded to the post-high-school survey.

Reprinted by permission of Mike Luckovich and Creators Syndicate.

When the data were compared for aggression at third and thirteenth grades and watching of television violence at those same grades, several statistically significant correlations were found. The strongest correlation was between aggressiveness at the two ages. For both boys and girls, those who were aggressive at third grade were more likely to be aggressive in the thirteenth grade. For the boys, two additional statistically significant correlations were noted. Watching violent television in the third grade was correlated to aggressiveness in the third grade and even more strongly correlated to aggressiveness in the thirteenth grade. . . .

META-ANALYSIS

One criticism of the scientific data generally is that many of the studies are of limited significance or that, while they demonstrate a relationship between violent viewing and aggression, the size of any effect is minor. Another criticism is that the conclusion that there is a causal relation, or even that a correlation exists, is based on only a subset of the studies done. There is a concern that studies that do not establish such a link go unpublished. If such work goes unpublished, it could be due to a bias on the part of journal editors, but it may only be the result of the conclusions that can be drawn from statistical studies. . . .

An approach to addressing the problems of significance and unreported studies may be found in meta-analysis. Meta-analysis is a quantitative review of the studies contained in the scholarly literature, providing an objective synthesis of the research. The method requires an examination of all the available studies, rather than basing its conclusions on certain selected studies. Such an examination provides better evidence as to the size of the effect of any of the variables studied and allows for comparisons of results based on the methods employed in the subject studies. A meta-analysis may also provide for greater certitude in the conclusions drawn. While one may still question the results of a single study, even when the results are statistically significant, an analysis that shows such a result consistently, from study to study and from method to method, would seem more difficult to question.

A 1990 meta-analysis by Professors George Comstock and Haejung Paik examined almost 200 methodologically sound studies on the relationship between violent television programming and aggressive behavior. The study included both published studies and unpublished work, such as dissertations, in an attempt to include all the available data. Their statistical analysis of that large body of data purported to eliminate the likelihood of publication bias. Based on the meta-analysis, the authors concluded that the data gathered in all the studies of the subject shows that television violence increases aggressive behavior. A later and larger sample meta-analysis, by the same researchers, produced similar results. . . .

CAUSE AND EFFECT

While the combination of results from the various forms of study seem to provide solid evidence for a causal relationship, there are those who would question the existence of such a causal effect in television. Television executives deny any such effect. Even those who do assert such an effect are only willing to conclude that television is *a* cause of violence in society. The questions over effect size indicate that there is more to the issue than television alone. Even throwing in films and video games will not account for all societal violence, but again that is not the claim of those who would impose some control. In the view of those who would regulate, even the effect size that has been established is cause for concern.

What is interesting is the fact that the television executive can argue that there is no causal effect and not seem disingenuous. It is true that all the psychological evidence can establish is a correlation between viewing televised violence and aggressiveness, and correlation is not the same as causation. The two correlated behaviors may both be caused by a third behavior or experience, or the correlation may be coincidental, but this is a possibility made less likely as more evidence is gathered and the statistical significance of the results becomes greater.

This difference between correlation and causation is of interest in areas other than social science and psychology. As the philosopher David Hume pointed out, we can never experience cause and effect. When we look for cause and effect, we instead experience constant conjunction. Even in as common an experience as striking a match on a dry, abrasive surface and observing that each time the match lights, all we have really observed is that, when the first event occurs, the second also occurs. Even despite this inability to experience directly the cause-and-effect relation, we nonetheless seem comfortable in asserting such a relation based on constant, or even almost-constant, conjunction in this sort of case.

SEARCHING FOR CAUSES

The evidence gathered in psychological studies may leave us less comfortable in jumping from correlation to causation. One factor in this reluctance is the fact that the conjunction present in psychology falls far short of constancy. That, however, cannot be the major factor. In the case of cigarettes and lung cancer, there is also a lack of constancy in the conjunction. Yet, the television executive who denies the aggression-causing effect of televised violence does not seem as disingenuous as the tobacco company executive who claims that there is no evidence that cigarettes cause lung cancer. Further, this difference does not seem explainable simply in terms of effect size. Lung cancer may be more likely to follow a life of smoking than homicide is to follow a childhood of viewing televised violence, but all that can be asserted of either cigarettes or television violence is that it is *a* cause. With cigarettes other environmental factors and genetics play a role, and with televised violence it is also clear that environmental factors, such as the child's upbringing, play a strong role.

The real difference between the ability to deny the causative effect of televised violence and the seeming unreasonableness of denying the causative effect of tobacco would seem to be in the ability to propose an explanatory chain of *physical* events. It is relatively simple to understand, at least in lay terms, how the irritation caused by tobacco smoke could cause changes in the lungs leading to cancer. For most people, psychology is simply lacking as a hard science capable of providing such physical explanations. Without such an offer of a physical chain of events, the skeptic seems more reasonable in denying a causal effect. There is now, however, work in brain science that might provide such a physical explanation.

VIOLENCE IN RATS

Professor Paul Mandel of the University of Strasbourg and his research group have studied the roles of neurotransmitters in the brains of rats. They focused on serotonin and on gamma-amino-butyric acid, or GABA. The studies involving GABA are particularly interesting in that they show that GABA serves as an inhibitor playing a role in violent behavior. Mandel worked with strains of rats that, through observation, showed to be particularly violent or particularly passive. For example, the Norway rats he used were more than three times more likely to kill than the Wistar rats he also used. When he studied the brains of rats from these various strains, he found that the GABA levels in the olfactory bulbs of the brains of the killer-rat strains were lower than the levels in non-killer-rat strains. He further found that the injection of GABA into the olfactory bulbs suppressed the killing behavior of these killer rats.

Mandel's work establishes a physical basis, at least in rats, for differences in violent behavior. Rats with lower levels of GABA are more violent than rats with higher base levels of GABA, and if rats low in GABA are given GABA injections they become less violent. Of more direct interest to the media-violence issue, it is reported that Professor Mandel also showed that the GABA levels in rats dropped when the rat observed other animals engaged in aggressive activity; that is, when a rat saw another rat kill a mouse, the observer rat's GABA level dropped. Since the drop in GABA level is physically tied to violence, the conclusion is indicated that violence can be contagious and watching violence makes a rat more violent.

A STEP IN ESTABLISHING CAUSATION

While the work described was with rats, and rats differ from humans, the physical basis for the relation between viewing violence and becoming aggressive in rats may make the conclusion that there is cause and effect in humans, rather than only correlation, more compelling. There may still be questions over the degree of correlation and the effect size, but humans have social inhibitors in addition to neurochemical inhibitors, so the regularity and size of the relation should not approach that in rats. Even accepting the rat studies as evidence of human brain activity, causation is not as established to the degree that it is in striking a match. It is, however, a step in establishing causation to the degree that it is established for tobacco and lung cancer.

The evidence seems strong that viewing violent television causes aggression. While it may still be argued that there is room for debate, even in 1981 [Donald Roberts and Christine Bachen wrote that] "the general consensus seem[ed] to be that there is a positive, causal relationship between television violence and subsequent aggressive behavior." Since that time, the evidence for a causal relationship, of some effect size, has not been shaken. As Senator Kent Conrad said in introducing his bill, *The Children's Media Protection Act of 1995,* " [t]he scientific debate is over. . . . [There is] convincing evidence that the observation of violence as seen in standard, every day television entertainment, does affect the aggressive behavior of the viewer."

"There is no scientific basis for
assuming [media violence] plays a
major role in the development of
aggression, and history provides
countless examples of whole societies
that became extraordinarily good at
aggression before the advent of the
movies or television."

TELEVISION VIOLENCE DOES NOT CAUSE SOCIETAL VIOLENCE

Kevin Durkin

In the following viewpoint, Kevin Durkin analyzes the research
regarding the link between television violence and real-world
violence. He argues that case studies, experimental studies, and
correlational studies all have serious flaws and have failed to
prove that television violence substantially contributes to violent
behavior among viewers. Durkin is a professor of psychology at
the University of Western Australia and author of *Developmental Social Psychology: From Infancy to Old Age.*

As you read, consider the following questions:

1. According to the author, what are the limitations of case
   studies?
2. On what basis does Durkin criticize the correlational study
   conducted by Leonard Eron and L. Rowell Huesmann?
3. What responses to television violence does Durkin
   recommend as alternatives to censorship?

Reprinted from Kevin Durkin, "Chasing the Effects of Media Violence," *ABA Update:
Newsletter of the Australian Broadcasting Authority*, March 1995, by permission of the author.

"The provision of media services is changing so rapidly in the final years of the twentieth century that it would be hazardous to attempt to predict what kinds of facilities will be available in just a few years' time."

One thing which can be reliably predicted is that some aspects of content will be deplored. In particular, we will be debating the perennial topics of violence, sex and bad language, the most frequently identified sources of complaint in most surveys of public reactions to broadcast television in this country and overseas.

It is also a pretty safe prediction that the world itself will be in a bad way. There will be plenty of violence, sex and bad language out there in reality as well as in our symbolic, entertainment versions. Could there be a connection, and should we be doing something about it now?

For many, the connection is obvious. In surveys of parents, for example, about 70 per cent tend to agree, or agree strongly, that television violence causes aggressive behaviour in children. Many politicians express strong concerns about media violence, and there is a consensus among psychologists that viewing media violence and developing a propensity to aggressive behaviour are linked. . . . Do these concerns and convictions mean that we should look very carefully at the evidence about media violence effects?

LISTENING TO THE RHETORIC

It is difficult to refute the conclusion that we should look carefully at the evidence, but in fact that is rarely undertaken. By and large, people prefer to listen to the rhetoric, perhaps because it is easier to grasp or perhaps because it tells us what we would like to hear—what we "know in our hearts" to be true. It seems so obvious that violent dramatizations in the media lead viewers into horrible imitations, that they desensitize children to violence, that they perpetuate aggression as a means of problem solving. The trouble is that the evidence does not show this at all.

There have been more than one thousand published studies of the effects of television violence and so far the results have been inconclusive. The work that has been done varies from the rigorous and ingenious to the pedestrian and silly, but it has not provided any evidence of substantial effects—and, in fact, most specialists in the field acknowledge this.

There are several different methodologies used in research into television violence, but the most common are case studies, experiments and correlational field studies.

THE LIMITATIONS OF CASE STUDIES

Case studies, or similar types of highly speculative anecdotal evidence, are often lent prominence in lay discussions, presumably because they provide vivid illustration of a seemingly straightforward story. Recent examples include the Bundy case in the U.S. (a convicted serial killer and rapist who attributed his path into crime as being due to pornography), the Strathfield case in New South Wales, Australia, (where a random mass killer was suspected of having viewed the film *Taxi Driver*) and the Bulger case in Britain (in which the judge suggested that media violence must have been part of the explanation of the behaviour [of two ten-year-old boys who murdered two-year-old Jamie Bulger]).

In each instance, an horrendous crime or series of crimes was committed; in each case, some link to media experiences was conjectured, by the accused, by the press, or by the presiding judge. In none of the cases is the evidence persuasive.

In fact, these case studies exhibit very clearly the limitations which lead most scientists to reject them as a source of conclusive evidence. First, they do not separate relevant factors systematically. For example, we are unable to test whether the offenders would have committed similar atrocities even after a viewing diet restricted exclusively to *Sesame Street*. Second, the sample is not representative of the population. The subject is selected because he or she is a problem, not because he or she is a typical viewer or consumer.

Third, some individuals may be motivated to represent the media as a source of their problems because this is preferable to accepting personal responsibility. Ted Bundy, for example, provided an eloquent and impassioned account of his views of the effects of pornography upon his own character, but he was at the time facing trial for a string of appalling crimes; his feelings about the adverse effects of media influence appeared to intensify as his execution approached.

MAKING A GOOD STORY

Finally, case studies are vulnerable to the influence of the investigator, or creative journalists, who may seek to find certain causes irrespective of the subject's responses. The Bulger tragedy provides an illustration of the risks of over-interpretation, or downright mischief with the facts. Here, little evidence was presented in court to support the inference of media effects.

Neither the police nor the prosecution made claims of media influence, there was no evidence that either child had watched the infamous *Child's Play III*, and experts who studied the film concluded that there was in any case little similarity between the events depicted in it and the details of the murder. The main piece of evidence used by the media was that one of the boys was said to hide his face whenever anything violent appeared on the television.

Rather more extensive evidence was provided that each boy was profoundly disturbed, had a long history of antisocial behaviour and grew up in a severely discordant family. It is possible that the judge had reached his conclusion about the undesirability of much contemporary television content before hearing this case, and it is possible that the international press was eager to seize upon any hint of television or video effects because these usually make a good story.

THE LIMITATIONS OF EXPERIMENTAL STUDIES

Many of the best known studies of the effects of violent television upon children are experimental, and this is the preferred method of many psychologists working in this field. A properly conducted experiment ensures that the variables of interest are controlled systematically. The experiment can determine exactly the conditions under which the subjects are exposed to the 'treatment' (e.g. viewing a particular program) and compare their responses with those of subjects exposed to other treatments, or not exposed to any. Measures can be defined precisely and collected rigorously.

Even so, there are limits to the kinds of evidence experiments can provide. One of the principal weaknesses of many experiments is that they are conducted under conditions which differ from real life experiences. For example, subjects in a research room might complete a questionnaire and then view a film, either alone or with a group of other subjects who are instructed not to speak to each other, and then complete another questionnaire. It is possible that these departures from normal viewing experiences may themselves incur departures from normal viewing behaviour and reactions.

Another problem is that the subjects might be influenced by what they perceive as the point of the exercise. Even quite young children are good at working out what adults want them to do, or will let them get away with. For example, in the classic "Bobo doll" studies introduced by Albert Bandura and colleagues in the early 1960s, preschoolers watch a filmed or live adult model violently work out his or her frustrations on a robust inflatable toy. The children are then subjected to mild frustration themselves and left in a room with the Bobo doll. They "attack" the Bobo doll, rather gleefully. Well, what would you do? Note that the doll is inanimate—even a four-year-old knows perfectly well that it does not suffer pain. Unlike real antagonists, the Bobo doll does not hit back. And finally, the children often appear to be enjoying themselves (their faces are lit up with pleasure). In real aggression in the playgrounds there is no fun, and faces are deadly serious.

THE LIMITATIONS OF CORRELATIONAL STUDIES

Correlational studies involve measuring the relationship between two or more variables. For example, the investigator might be interested in the effects of amount of television viewing on young people's aggressive behaviour. From a sample of young people he or she might collect a measure of how much television each individual watches per week, and a measure of his or her aggression in simulated or real circumstances, e.g. as rated by parents, peers or teachers. An attraction of this methodology is that it focuses upon naturally occurring behaviours, e.g. amount of television viewed, rather than laboratory-induced activities.

One problem is that because subjects are not allocated at random to different conditions, differences between groups could be due to any one or more confounding variables. For example, highly aggressive individuals might choose to watch a lot of television violence. If we find a correlation between these two variables, it is difficult to determine which came first. Another possibility is that both variables may be correlated with a third, and the third may actually be the more important. For example, high television viewing in children is correlated with lax parenting; aggressive behaviour in children is also correlated with lax parenting; hence, it is possible that the real source of problems is family management.

Some of these problems can be addressed in sophisticated designs and by use of appropriate statistical techniques. One of the best attempts to do so is a well-known longitudinal study initiated by Leonard Eron and L. Rowell Huesmann in 1960, in which the investigators attempted to track the viewing interests and aggressive behaviour of a large sample of children growing up in New York State. This was an ambitious project which aimed to investigate the statistical relations among early aggression, early viewing, later aggression and later viewing.

PEER-RATED AGGRESSION

The main finding concerns a sub-sample of boys, studied at ages 8 and 18. The researchers found no relationship between peer-rated aggression at age 8 and preference for television violence at age 18. However, they did find a relationship between preference for violent television at age 8 and aggressiveness ratings at age 18. No such relationships were found for girls. The researchers interpret their findings as lending "considerable support to the hypothesis that preferring to watch violent television is a cause of aggressive behavior."

There are some limitations to the study in terms of measures and subject loss across the duration. A crucial problem concerns the measure of peer-rated aggression (central to the claim above). Here, children rated their peers on items such as "did not listen to the teacher," "gave dirty looks or made unfriendly gestures to other students," "used to say mean things," "started fights over nothing," "pushed or shoved other students." Clearly, these set the terms of "aggression" rather generously. A skeptic might say that the study pointed to a relationship between preferring to watch violent television and giving dirty looks or saying mean things—a worrying phenomenon, to be sure, but perhaps not the firmest basis for media regulation.

Rather more weight might be given to starting fights and pushing and shoving, but only by people who have never queued for school dinner. We are not looking at miniature Ted Bundys in this sample, and some of the claims that have been made on the basis of this evidence are simply farfetched. More interesting is an extension of the study to when the male subjects had reached the age of 30 when some had acquired criminal records. There was a slight association between preference for television violence at age 8 and commission of violent crime by age 30. There was also a slight association between rated aggressiveness at age 8 and violent crime at age 30. In the latest report, Huesmann and M. Miller are careful to stress that these data are based on small numbers of subjects, the minority of their sample who became criminals. Most of the high early viewers of violent television did not grow up to become violent criminals.

In short, each of the principal means of investigation of the effects of violent television content has its drawbacks and, quite properly, research into such a complex topic will inevitably be open to criticism. However, even if we accept the findings of the most prominent research, such as Eron and Huesmann's, they tell us that the relationship between viewing and aggressive behaviour is a weak one. Nobody has ever demonstrated otherwise. Huesmann and Miller acknowledge that many other factors must be involved in the explanation of aggressive behaviour.

CENSORSHIP BY GUT FEELING

So, what can we conclude on the basis of these necessarily weak findings? Surely caution is warranted?

An understandable reaction to the continuing debate over the nature of television violence effects is to reason: "Well, the effects may or may not be proven, but aggression is certainly a major human problem and anything we can do to avoid the risks of inciting it must be a good thing." Hence, let us err on the side of caution, and ban some or all television violence.

This is an honest argument: honest, but censorial. It is honest to admit that one is proceeding on gut intuition rather than research evidence. However, gut feeling is a precarious basis for censorship, and censorship is a dramatic process to instigate in a democratic society. Whose guts do we trust? Where do we stop?

The problem is by no means trivial. While I might find in the antics of Tom and Jerry the most reprehensible exhibition of interspecies physical disregard, you might feel it's just harmless fun that even a kindergartner can see is not for real. Moving up to adult programs, a filmed attack which I might find distressing and therefore seek to ban, might in your view be conveying an important message. Perhaps the theme of the program is that ultimately violence is futile, or its purpose might be to expose the maltreatment of oppressed members of our community and the unpleasant scene is actually being used for dramatic effect in a compelling message. My gut feeling says "ban it"; yours says, "hold on, the issue here is worth discussing." But discussion's out, remember—we thought it was best to err on the side of caution.

Well, it's a pity about discussion, because research into families and television has tended to show it is a good thing: parents can mitigate negative effects and promote positive effects. In fact, it is well known to developmental psychologists that discussions between parent and child are the primary locus for learning about social values, moral standards, personal aspirations. Television, like any other shared experience, can be used within families as a topic for discussion. If you wanted to talk to your children about the dangers of city life, would you prefer to take off from a mugging in 21 Jump Street or wait until there was a real one down your street? By ensuring that nothing that might be seen as offensive, disturbing or provocative could ever be shown on our screens, we can probably make at least a minor contribution towards undermining the scope for family discussions.

MAKING INFORMED VIEWING DECISIONS

Does this mean advocating a free-for-all with absolutely no safeguards standing between children and the vilest of media imagery? Not at all. For one thing, we remain at liberty to criticize. There is much on our television screens to encourage us to practice this skill. It is healthy, in a democratic society, to do so, just as it is healthy, in a democratic family, to express feelings and beliefs. We also have procedures and the potential to improve those procedures—whereby parents and children can receive information about upcoming program content which can help them make informed viewing decisions. This is called classification, a fraught but essentially much more democratic service than censorship. New technologies are coming which will even enable parents to restrict reception of certain types of program content, and many may judge this a useful, if imperfect, option. And we retain that old piece of decisive technology, the "off" button.

Of course, not all children are raised in families in which parents have the time, skills and motivation to monitor their television experiences. Neglected and abused children are undoubtedly at greater risk, but it is not possible to maintain a serious argument that all television content should be regulated in accord with the viewing needs of neglected children. Television is a diverse community resource, used by people in myriad circumstances for wide-ranging purposes. It could certainly be improved, but improvement will not be accelerated by gearing all content to what experts judge suitable for child victims. For their part, child victims do merit urgent community assistance, but better to deliver it to them rather than imagine that censorship will somehow cure all, or any, of the stresses they face in unsatisfactory homes.

The evidence of effects of media violence upon behaviour is controversial but, at best, weak. There is no scientific basis for assuming it plays a major role in the development of aggression, and history provides countless examples of whole societies that became extraordinarily good at aggression before the advent of the movies or television. The most potent weapons we have for combating aggression in the real world are community debate, scientific research, imagination and resourcefulness and goodwill—far preferable to the careless exaggeration of weak evidence, followed by the dull thud of censorship, and finished off with a diet of politically correct viewing.

| "When [prominent industry leaders] talk about 'pushing the envelope,' they really mean filling it."

TELEVISION IS CORRUPTING AMERICAN SOCIETY

Joe McNamara

In the following viewpoint, Joe McNamara argues that television and Hollywood are both morally bankrupt. To illustrate his point, he describes episodes of *Seinfeld* and *The Simpsons*, which he says demonstrate a callous disregard for human dignity and moral standards. In addition, he contends that studies have shown that viewing media violence causes acts of physical aggression. McNamara is the executive director of marketing communications at Hillsdale College in Michigan.

As you read, consider the following questions:

1. How does the author respond to the claim that television violence is "not real"?
2. What evidence does McNamara give for his claim that humor has long been used to undermine traditional values?
3. What should viewers do to help reverse the trend of vulgarity, according to the author?

Reprinted from Joe McNamara, "Anything Goes: Moral Bankruptcy of Television and Hollywood," *USA Today* magazine, January 1998, by permission of the Society for the Advancement of Education.

In 1961, Newton N. Minow, chairman of the Federal Communications Commission, challenged executives of the television industry "to sit down in front of your television set when your station goes on the air and stay there without a book, magazine, newspaper, profit-and-loss sheet or rating book to distract you—and keep your eyes glued to that set until the station signs off. I can assure you that you will observe a vast wasteland. . . .

"Is there one person in this room who claims that broadcasting can't do better? Your trust accounting with your beneficiaries is overdue."

More than three decades later, an intelligent teenage viewer laughs uncontrollably as a dog gnaws on a brain growing outside the head of a young man, who then embraces a number of women dressed in white, spattering them with blood. When asked why he's laughing, the viewer—my son—replies, "Because it's funny."

HORSES OUT OF THE BARN

Jerry Seinfeld claims that dropping candy into an incision in an operating room after saying, "All right, just let me finish my coffee and we'll go watch them slice this fat bastard up," was a turning point on Seinfeld because, "Once that happened, it was like the horses were out of the barn. We thought, if we can get away with this . . .". The series' acme, according to critic Jay McInerney (who called the episode "brilliant"), involved doing an entire show about masturbation without ever referring to it by name as "four friends compete to see who can remain 'master of [their] domain' the longest."

In a bowling alley, Homer Simpson's decapitated head rolls slowly down the lane towards pins impaled with spikes, driving one of them into the skull, which pops open to reveal a note: "I owe you one brain. Signed, God." Bart Simpson's grace before meals runs, "Hey, God, we did all this ourselves, so thanks for nothing." Lisa Simpson mockingly describes prayer as "the last refuge of the scoundrel."

To all of these incidents, and countless others, my 12-year-old son, with the nodding agreement of his three brothers, proclaims: "Don't worry, Dad, none of that is real; it's just television."

Yet, it is real, very real, and much, much more than "just television." For those in their early teens, it is seeing 15,000 sexual acts or innuendoes and a total of 33,000 murders and 200,000 acts of random violence in a single year, according to the American Family Association.

While more than 3,000 studies have documented the inexorable nexus between TV violence and socially aggressive behavior, no one has described the relationship between humor and disappearing moral standards, though the behavioral keys involved are identical. According to psychologists, these are observational learning (attention, retention, motivation, and potential reproduction) and the selection of a model one chooses to imitate.

Studies conducted in Oak Park, Mich., in 1977 and followed up in 1992 showed that "women who watched violent television shows as children in the 1970s are more physically aggressive and more capable of committing criminal acts today." The women who scored at the top of categories "watched aggressive female heroines in the media as children and continued to do so as adults." These results "confirmed some of our worst fears," indicates L. Rowell Huesmann, a psychology professor and researcher in the Aggression Research Group at the University of Michigan Institute for Social Research, Ann Arbor.

Another study by the same institute documented the rise of and rationale for play-ground bullies. After studying the viewing habits of a group of children for 30 years, the researchers concluded that TV violence desensitizes the very young and noted that television "played a larger role in children's aggression than poverty, race, or parental behavior."

ABUSING CHILDREN FOR PROFIT

Demeaning an important American art form may be bad enough, but abusing children to make a profit at the same time defies comprehension. Syndicated columnist Suzanne Fields noted that "Our children face an unusual enemy of childhood today, grown-ups who conduct a carpet bombing of information and images against kids who simply don't have the maturity to understand what they see and hear." Understand it they may not, but enjoy it they do, and remarkably few major critics—with the exception of Diane and Michael Medved; William Bennett; columnists Bob Herbert and Kirk Nicewonger; and Harvard University's Alvin F. Pouissant—will say a word.

Humor has become a form of psychological violence, but Hollywood's lethal silence among the writers, producers, studios, and critics who lack the courage to face the truth and do what is right remains virtually intact. There are, after all, millions of dollars to be made in exploiting the vulnerabilities of children whose values are not yet formed and who are looking for leadership and role models.

In the case of situation comedies, their laughter directed towards premarital or extramarital sex constitutes positive reinforcement with documentable—some would say detestably corrosive—consequences. Apparently, the worst mistake young men or women can make involves choosing abstinence when everything around them reflects the sexual obsession that supposedly typifies life in America.

"With sex-starved Amandas and out-of-the-closet 'Friends' crowding early prime time, would homespun TV characters stand a chance today?" asks *TV Guide*, already knowing the answer. *Friends* has the concept of the traditional family squarely and effectively in its sights. *Living Single* offers racial and ethnic stereotypes that might even shock Archie Bunker, as well as the thousands who have invested their lives in something called the civil rights movement. The characters on *Melrose Place*, as someone once said of an oft-married Hollywood figure, "could find sex in the crotch of a tree." *Melrose Place* producer Frank South, choosing an unfortunate metaphor for his show's promotion of homosexuality, says, "We'll keep pushing." Do the songs of fools now outweigh the rebukes of the wise? Check out "sweeps" months and find out.

HOLLYWOOD'S DOUBLE STANDARD

In fact, Hollywood's advocacy of gays and lesbians exposes a glaring double standard. The author of *The Celluloid Closet* proudly boasts that "Hollywood . . . taught straight people what to think about gay people and gay people what to think about themselves. No one escaped its influence." United Features Syndicate critic Kirk Nicewonger notes, "Aren't many of those who would nod solemnly in agreement with these sentiments the same people who scoff at concerns about movie violence influencing real-life behavior?" Humor influences as well and perhaps more effectively because it is not perceived as a form of violence or even as attempted influence.

By 1980, the out-of-wedlock birth rate reached a total of 18% of annual births and then jumped to slightly over 30% by 1992. While the percentages are frightening enough, the real numbers are numbing: in 1992, 1,224,876 babies were born to single women, and white females between the ages of 20 and 30 constitute the fastest-growing group. At this rate, by 2015, 50% of all children born will be born out of wedlock. No *Murphy Brown* this, but the reflection of a generally acidic attitude toward the traditional views of marriage and morality.

Situation comedies cannot be singled out as the sole cause of such a decline, but the attitudes they spawn and constantly reinforce contribute directly to the problem. Researcher Robert Maginnis reports that, when individuals between the ages of 18 and 30 were "asked to assess the degree to which today's movies, television, and music lyrics encourage teenage sex," 63% said "a great deal" or "quite a lot."

HUMOR AS INSTINCT

Raunchily destructive comic attitudes toward traditional virtues and families did not assume center stage overnight. For centuries, laughter was seen as a method of teaching, following French playwright Moliere's belief that the comic sought "to correct through amusement." Philosopher Jean-Jacques Rousseau, according to author J.Y.T. Grieg, thought that "comedy performed no useful social function even at its best, and might at its worst lead directly to corruption and immorality."

Yet, Grieg also mentions, and partially endorses, Max Eastman's *The Sense of Humor*. Eastman sees humor as an instinct and claims that there is "a certain range of feelings which can be enjoyed playfully, just as certain wave-lengths can be perceived as light, and if you pass beyond this laugh spectrum at either end the humor disappears." He goes on to assert that "Aggression jokes derive their peculiar delightfulness from the fact that we have cruel impulses which we cannot unleash in serious life, cultural standards being here at variance with our instincts, and they sneak forth and take a drink of satisfaction when we play." Moreover, "Jests often liberate the surging wishes prisoned in us. They remove the lid of our culture, and let us be, in fun at least and for a second, animals."

Traditional cultural standards do supply the guidelines that make civilized life possible and safe, sometimes even despite our own instincts. However, when Eastman sees the function of comedy as some sort of relief valve which can "remove the lid of our culture" and allow us to be animals "in fun at least and for a second," he has put his finger on the dilemma. The second has been stretched into minutes, to half-hour shows, to entire years of television production, and, for some, to a way of life.

BRUTAL VULGARIZATIONS

Humor as a basically harmless interchange between equals has given way to brutal vulgarizations with no end in sight. As Rabbi Daniel Lapin of Toward Tradition once explained to me, if a British barrister falls down once, it may be funny. Repeated falls, though, must contain increasingly bizarre elements to keep the audience "entertained." The same may be said for American humor and its attendant profanity and vulgarity, set on a deliberately downward course by writers, directors, executives, and actors. The real matter here is money, and some in the entertainment industry, driven by fear of failure, will do anything, even—or perhaps especially—to vulnerable children, to boost the bottom line.

Screenwriter John Gregory Dunne's lunch with a Hollywood producer took an odd turn when the producer pretended to grab a small animal from under the table and asked Dunne if he saw "the monster" and recognized it. Stunned, Dunne replied that he neither could see nor name the imaginary animal, and the producer exclaimed, "It's our money." Dunne describes the resultant six years, four contracts, and 27 drafts of one movie script in his book, *Monster: Living Off the Big Screen*. The script concerned the tortured life of TV newswoman Jessica Savitch, up to her drowning in the muck of the Delaware Canal. The finished version, six years later, "though it bore absolutely no resemblance to the raw material from which it had been wrenched, did what [the Disney studio] wanted it to do: It made money, thereby feeding the monster."

THE PLAGUE OF PESSIMISM

Apparently, Hollywood has little or no compunction about feeding kids to the monster. Michael and Diane Medved's book, *Saving Childhood: How to Protect Your Children from the National Assault on Innocence*, argues forcefully that youngsters need to be protected from the pessimism that dominates television and motion pictures. The Medveds acknowledge the inevitability of observational learning: "The deepest problem with this material isn't the possibility that children will imitate the behavior they see on screen, though we know that this sort of imitation does occur. The more universal threat involves the underlying message conveyed by these ugly, consistently dysfunctional images, encouraging self-pity and fear." Although they refer here to Hollywood's staccato drumbeat that things always will get worse, they base their conclusions on the notion that "prolonged exposure to the dysfunctional elements in our culture" will cause viewers to "lose faith, confidence and resistance . . . to the plague of pessimism."

More often than not, situation comedies celebrate dysfunctionality by rejecting the very things that make civilized life possible: discipline, self-control, hard work, delayed gratification, faith, and a commitment to genuine families. Yet, one network executive recently claimed: "Little by little, everybody has gotten a little less afraid of the old taboos. . . . It seems we're able to go a lot further than we have, even considering the conservative swing the country has taken." These executives have ravaged the roots of cultural traditions, professing not dismay, but dollar-driven self-satisfaction at the moral mud-slides that inevitably follow such deliberate destruction of America's religious roots.

The writers and producers responsible for such destruction could give their audiences much more, but they choose not to. They have opted for the dollar-laden low road, competing to see who can get away with the most first, afraid not to follow the pack for fear of being characterized as out of step with Hollywood leadership. Instead of intelligence, integrity, and inspiration, viewers get what one producer ordered: "We were told to lose the contrived plot stuff . . . and [add] . . . more big hair and breasts." What drives some of the most talented people in the world to such demi-moronic nihilism? These very same people have shown, time and again, they can produce laughter combined with sophistication and optimism, but they will not. Instead, we get the boobonic plague.

CHEAP, EASY, AND MORONIC

There are exceptions, but their ranks are thinning. Actor Michael J. Fox won't let his own children watch his new show, *Spin City*. Everyone in the industry could learn a lesson from director Spike Lee: "Sometimes art should be about elevation, not just wallowing in the same old [crap]. . . . Life is valued cheaply. I definitely wanted to offer another view."

Given time, however, those writers and executives who lower the level of intelligence and discourse with brainless sex, profanity, nudity, and vulgarity have anesthetized, and eventually will annihilate, the ability of an audience to react positively to anything higher or ennobling. "I don't think audiences know how to be audiences anymore," producer Norman Lear told Nancy Hass of *The New York Times*. "They just want to hoot and make sounds." Lear still doesn't get it, because he insists that television's sexual saturation is not a moral issue: "The biggest problem with how much sex there is on TV isn't whether it's offensive. . . . It's that most [of it] just isn't funny. It's stupid and boring." Hass agrees that "many people within the industry—and no doubt many viewers" think that the real issue is variety, not morality. No wonder she entitled her article, "Cheap, Easy, and Moronic."

Prominent industry leaders know they are destroying the medium for those who will follow, but they simply refuse to acknowledge that reality. When they talk about "pushing the envelope," they really mean filling it. The money's too good and the audience too easy to exploit, so executives, writers, and producers follow the very same predatory practices that they, in their scripts and lives, usually attribute to business executives and religious figures. Favorite targets include corporate officials, Roman Catholic priests and nuns, and evangelical leaders.

We have gone from stand-up comics Mort Sahl and Lenny Bruce to the literate sophistication of Mike Nichols and Elaine May, through roundly mocked, "sugar-coated" Jackie Gleason and Lucille Ball to the brainless profanity of Dennis Miller and sexually laden and insulting racist, ethnic, and religious stereotypes. Humor on many shows has become a form of cultural and psychological violence, but no one looks at it that way because vulnerable young audiences respond, corporate sponsors chuckle and congratulate themselves, and everyone associated with the industry laughs all the way to the bank.

A half-mile wide and 27 miles long, Malibu, Calif., justifiably can claim that "nowhere in the world is there such a concentration of wealth and stardom," a belief few would refute. Those five beaches and six canyons hold the future of an art form with a generation of viewers and an important aspect of America's cultural integrity in them, but the occupants are in debt and refuse to admit it. An entire generation of youngsters has been taken hostage and doesn't know it. There will be no ransom note, only commercials from corporations who apparently care more about market share than our children's future.

A Vast Wasteland

No one has the courage to offer the "trust accounting" demanded by Newton Minow more than 35 years ago or to address his most recent concerns: "In 1961, I worried that my children would not benefit much from television, but in 1991, I worry that my grandchildren will actually be harmed by it. . . . In 1961, they didn't make PG-13 movies, much less NC-17. Now, a six-year-old can watch them on cable."

In his 1991 Gannett Foundation Media Center revisiting of the "vast wasteland" speech of 1961, Minow quoted journalist E.B. White's reaction in 1938 when he first saw the new technological then-oddity called television: "We shall stand or fall by television, of that I am sure. I believe television is going to be the test of the modern world, and that in this new opportunity to see beyond the range of our vision, we shall discover there either a new and unbearable disturbance to the general peace, or a saving radiance in the sky."

Must television and motion pictures remain Minow's "reactive mirror of the lowest common denominator" of society? Must the men and women invested with such power pursue only their dollar-denominated death-spiral? Must they continue to degrade, deny, and eventually destroy White's "new opportunity to see beyond the range of our vision"? Must there be "a new and unbearable disturbance to the general peace" because those responsible for it haven't the courage to see the source of the disturbance in their Malibu mirrors? Imagine trying to justify applying the phrase "saving radiance in the sky" to the morals of today's situation comedies.

There is plenty viewers can do to protest this trend. Just three of the 25 best-selling videos of all times have an "R" rating. Go buy the other 22 and show them repeatedly. Watch many of the classics made before the first "R" rating in 1968, because 60% of the films made after that were "R" or worse. Look for the Dove Foundation's blue-and-white label on videos the Grand Rapids, Mich., organization rates as "family friendly," or sponsor a low-cost, multi-film festival they can help you set up.

Open that most radical of books, the Bible, and talk about the revelations of Revelation. Get some of the best of PBS, like *Shad-*

owlands and Ken Burns, and ignore most of the ideology-laden glop they throw at you. Explain to your kids that masterpieces teach you something new about yourself every time you see them, and then watch them again. Revisit older musicals and newer versions (after viewing the latter yourself first). Watch historical footage, especially of combat, with older kids, and explain that all this was done in the name of freedom. Convert your church social hall or service club to a mini-theater and offer a weekly film festival of your own. Keep cheesy film-gossip magazines out of your house and out of your life.

Work to establish a money-back guarantee at motion picture theaters. Most honest merchants have one. If you leave the movie within the first 20 minutes, you should have a right to get your money back because you were dissatisfied with what your ticket bought you.

The real trick is how to do this without seeming to be overbearing and out of touch with your children and their friends. There are usually no fanfares or overtures for unsung heroes. The best music comes later.

| "I slowly but surely became convinced
... that [television] was being
blamed for social changes that were
rooted in forces far, far more powerful
than the most ardent television
salesman would ever dare claim."

TELEVISION IS NOT CORRUPTING AMERICAN SOCIETY

Jeff Greenfield

In the following viewpoint, Jeff Greenfield argues that cultural forces, rather than television, are the source of much of what critics call "cultural decline." According to Greenfield, social and economic changes following World War II, including the advent of the birth control pill and increased prosperity and mobility, have brought about significant cultural changes. At the same time, television's declining standards and television producers' increasing willingness to air vulgar programs made television an easy scapegoat. Greenfield, a former speechwriter for Robert Kennedy, covers politics and the media for ABC News.

As you read, consider the following questions:

1. According to Greenfield, why did television come under attack in the early 1950s?
2. In what way is television an "incredibly subversive medium," according to the author?
3. According to Greenfield, what was significant about the 1950s television program *You Asked for It*?
4. What was the author's response to being targeted by the film crew from a television tabloid show?

From Jeff Greenfield, "The Business of Television News," in *Do the Media Govern?* edited by Shanto Iyengar and Richard Reeves. Copyright ©1997 by Sage Publications, Inc. Reprinted by permission of Sage Publications, Inc.

A s many of you know, there is a long tradition in this industry, and at gatherings such as these, which I have come to think of as the ritual mortification of the spirit at the hands of an angry prophet.

Year after year at gatherings of news directors and at convocations of publishers, editors, advertisers, reporters, correspondents, and other worthies, a speaker is invited to stand before a group such as this and decry the sure, steady descent to hell in a hand basket in which we—and you—are willing, eager passengers. I hope you will forgive me if that is an honor that, in one sense, I have chosen to decline.

Such a speaker notes the technological wonder of modern communications, invokes the potential glories of an enlightened civilization which communications once promised, deplores the current state of grubby commerce and shameless pandering to the public appetite, and hurls the lightning bolts down at the offending miscreants with the zeal of Reverend Jonathan Edwards calling down the wrath of heaven on sinners in the hands of an angry God. The speech ends, the speaker feels himself a cleansing agent, the audience feels purified. The speaker goes home, you go to lunch, end of assignation.

A Stench in the Nostrils

The tradition is so deeply rooted I suspect that some centuries ago a guest writer at the Fifth Annual Company Dinner of Gutenberg Printers decried the tawdry commercial ventures of moveable type. In 1958, Edward R. Murrow told a convention of radio and TV news directors that the networks were offering entirely too much of "decadence, escapism, and insulation from the realities of the world in which we live. And without courage and vision, television is nothing more than lights, and wires in a box." Three years after that, FCC Chairman Newt Minow invited members of the National Association of Broadcasters to sit down in front of their TV sets and told them that "you will observe a vast wasteland." It was in this spirit that Lee DeForest, inventor of the electron tube and one of the fathers of the television industry, said "you have debased my child. . . . You have made him a laughingstock of intelligence, a stench in the nostrils of the gods of the ionosphere."

So it is long since past time that those of us who toil in the Elysian Fields of network news stop the pretense that we somehow are above the tawdry compromises with commercialism, sensationalism, and pandering that afflict the lesser journalistic breeds. Somewhere between the cross-country chase for Tonya

Harding and Camp O.J., our virginal white has acquired more than a few hints of tattle-tale gray. Too often we sound like Claude Rains as the inspector in *Casablanca*, who was "shocked—shocked" to learn of gambling in Rick's establishment before the waiter rushed over to hand him his winnings.

If the networks are truly the last bastion of civilized restraint, then why are so many of these deplorable programs on the local stations that the networks themselves own and operate? If a sober, responsible network newscast ends at 6:58 p.m. and the latest slam-bang tabloid program begins two minutes later on the same network owned-and-operated station, then how much standing do we really have to proclaim that we are not part of that world?

MISPLACED ATTACKS

Television executives should at this point be asked a question—one wrapped not in the mantle of moral superiority, but in the more modest trappings of hard-nosed, practical, enlightened self-interest—why does the industry want to hand its critics a 12 pound lead cudgel with which to beat us over the head at a time when television is once again being attacked for things that are manifestly not the medium's fault? Why are we so anxious to provide supporting evidence for the most extreme, outlandish criticisms of television?

Let me be clear about what I mean: Long before I ever imagined that I would ever work on television, I was writing about it, its programs, and about its alleged impact on the political and social life of the nation. I slowly but surely became convinced that much of the attacks on television—attacks almost as old as television itself—were fundamentally misplaced; that the medium was being blamed for social changes that were rooted in forces far, far more powerful than the most ardent television salesman would ever dare claim.

In the early 1950s, the first congressional hearings were held that indicted TV for its alleged impact on the then-shocking emergence of juvenile delinquency. That kind of inquiry became a tradition, continued in the U.S. Senate by Senator Paul Simon of Illinois who considered proposing or imposing a variety of restrictions on TV, in the interests of curbing the epidemic of violence in the United States. And yet for all of the attacks on TV, all of the academic studies that counted every set of aggression from dramatized slaughter to the misadventures of Bugs Bunny and Daffy Duck, few ever bothered to look at what had happened in the United States not because of TV but coincident with and independent of TV.

An Uncertain Generation

This country uprooted itself after World War II. By the tens of millions we left the neighborhoods, the towns, the cities where we had been for generations. We left for better jobs, freedom, opportunity, excitement, for a new life. But with uprooting came upheaval; we were liberated not just from limited opportunity but from restraint, social contract, the guard rails of the extended family and neighborhood. And so crime and disorder rose, families fractured and the familiar faded, and our culture became not just more free but more uncertain.

Television did not do this to us.

Or consider: In the early 1960s television was very much a world where married couples slept in separate beds with enough night clothing to ward off an Arctic chill. As far as an alien viewer would be able to tell from the tube, human beings reproduced by parthenogenesis. At that time a pill came on the market that uncoupled sex from pregnancy for the first time in human history. And this at a time when the explosion in American prosperity had already given us more opportunity, for young people by the millions were going off to college on their own, no longer under parental control. That prosperity and mobility gave many women their first chance to think about whether a lifetime in marriage was their only possibility. And so the whole idea that sex must be confined to marriage weakened and premarital and extra-marital sex, always a reality, now became far more widespread and increasingly acceptable.

Television did not do this to us.

Or consider the changing nature of work combined with increasing opportunity for Americans once doomed to privation because of racial bigotry, which delivered a deadly one-two punch to our least well-off neighborhoods. Those with the education and the talent left for greener pastures. Those who remained found work harder and harder to find. And with that, as has happened in every afflicted community within memory, men without work found little to tie them to the whole concept of family, and with that disconnect came the whirlwind of children having children and epidemic violence that afflicts us today.

Television did not do this to us.

A Subversive Medium

So why do so many blame television for so much? Why do voices that agree with each other on almost nothing else unite to declare that television is not simply the messenger, but the carrier of so many social ills? Why do Senator Jesse Helms of

North Carolina and Senator Paul Simon, who would not agree on what day of the week it is, unite in their belief that television has helped bring us to our sorry state?

Part of the explanation is simple: timing. Television came into our homes just when the post war upheaval was beginning. So why not assume that, since television arrived with our growing national nervousness, television must have caused it?

"Is it any wonder there's so much violence today, when this kind of stuff is all our kids have to look at?"

From *The Wall Street Journal* by permission of Cartoon Features Syndicate.

Television was, is, and always has been an incredibly subversive medium. Subversive not in the sense that the late Senator Joseph McCarthy would have used the phrase, but in the fact that every new medium of communication is subversive because it undermines established ways of looking at things. If you were a traditional white Southerner in the 1950s, TV showed you a reality about black and white you never had to see before, and therefore never had to think about. If you were an American who knew only good things about our boys in uniform and our foreign adventures, television showed you a face of war you had never seen before. If you were a good-hearted liberal convinced that a government program could cure the ills of society, television showed you a heart of darkness and a harsh reality about the enduring nature of evil that no one liked.

And more generally, television was far more intrusive than other media because it poured out of the tube into your home in front of your family. As a viewer, you had little real control over what was coming at you. Industry voices pointed to the "on-off" switch, but this has always been a ludicrously weak argument—if something shocking or upsetting to you pops out of the tube—then it is too late for the "on-off" switch.

And consider: Conservatives get to dislike it because it comes out of Hollywood and New York, the two most despised communities for conservatives now that Moscow is no longer Communist. And it is sustained by big corporations in pursuit of profit, which means liberals get to hate it too. But there is another reason why the medium is blamed so eagerly for consequences it did not produce and lurking here is a real danger for our common enterprises. One of the reasons people believe that television is responsible for so many ills of our society is that we make it so easy for them to believe it with what we are willing to put on the air.

A FREAK SHOW MEDIUM

Why shouldn't people believe in television's capacity to contribute to societal breakdown when we prove every day that we can be supremely indifferent to the way we treat vulnerable and helpless human beings? Why shouldn't our critics believe that we don't care about the consequences of turning the pain and grief and rage of weak and hurting human beings into the modern-day equivalent of freak shows? The case grows even stronger when you consider the way we defend such programs. It would be one thing to say simply, "people watch them eagerly; they're cheap to produce; they get ratings; they make money." That would at least have the virtue of being honest.

But instead, we hear these arguments: "Oh, but people want to see these programs. It's the marketplace in action." Well of course they want to see them. If they didn't, there wouldn't be any argument at all, unless some demented programmer insisted that he was putting such programs on as a public service.

Back in the early days of television there was a popular program called You Asked For It. It was a program that answered viewers' requests for stunts of one kind or another. And do you know what the most requested segment—by far—was? It was for a televised execution. Television was a more elitist medium then, and the request was never honored. Sometimes, late at night, I conjure up a syndicator offering a new, updated version of You Asked For It in today's marketplace. It is not a pleasant thought.

Well, says the host of one of these popular syndicated offerings, it is a free speech issue; who are we to deny these people a chance to air their stories in public? Listening to such an argument makes it easier to understand how this particular host's former career as a politician ended when he had the bad judgment to employ the services of a prostitute and pay her with a check.

SENSE OF RESTRAINT AND DIGNITY

The question isn't whether there is a constitutional right for people to produce and participate in such programs. The question is—what are television executives doing producing such programs, airing them, and what are other corporations doing by sponsoring them? Given the legal right that television executives have to air such shows, the public has a right to draw their logical conclusions about TV's sense of restraint and common ordinary decency. What conclusion should the public draw regarding television's sincerity in its claim of serving the public interest?

Well, the argument goes, nobody is dragging these people in front of the camera; they are there because they want to be.

I want to give credit to the producers of these programs. They are skilled in finding people for whom the prospect of a free airplane ticket, a ride in a limo, a hotel suite with room service, and their first and last chance to be on television is a prize well worth the sacrifice of any shred of dignity and privacy. They are also skilled in convincing their "guests"—let's consider for a moment the irony of that term—to earn their free trip by hurling angry words and by sitting still for that surprise confrontation that audiences love so much. But now let me pose a different scenario for these shows, one that came to me when I became the target of one of the third-tier tabloid shows now sadly dispatched to that great curing-room in the sky.

CRIME AND PUNISHMENT

My sin was to decline, politely, an interview request by the show's anchor—a request delivered with the camera rolling about six inches from my face. My punishment was to be pursued by a young man with a hand-held video camera, screaming at me, demanding to know why I was "afraid" to talk to this show. Across the street, another camera was rolling, in case I had the bad judgment to physically assault my interrogator.

After the airing of this episode, I began to play with a revenge fantasy. It would do no good to go after the anchor or the producers, that would just make better television for them. Instead I imagined going to the offices and to the homes of the top officers and directors of the Chris-Craft Company—for it was their show. I thought of surrounding these people with two video cameras, jamming one of them in the face of the board chairman and demanding to know why he was willing to profit from the debasing of the American TV industry. If he refused to answer? Follow him for as long as I could demanding to know why he was afraid to talk to the American people.

From there the fantasy blossomed. I learned that many of the most noxious of these programs actually are produced and aired by some of our most well-respected, prominent organizations—huge media conglomerates run by people who spend half their evenings getting Humanitarian of the Year awards. Why not invite several of them on a show like *Nightline*, allegedly to talk about serious matters of telecommunications policy, or the social responsibility of business. Then, after careful research, we would stash backstage people from their past that they would really, really rather never see again.

People who knew something profoundly embarrassing about their lives. Odds are, they all have such a person in their past; God knows I do.

As we go on the air live we would bring out these guests and let them denounce our major corporate and communications leaders for whatever, preferably for sins of the most intimate, private sort. And we wouldn't even have to check their stories out all that carefully. After all, we have a First Amendment, don't we?

Or maybe we'd try a different kind of approach. Take a hidden camera and follow these important industry people everywhere they went. Maybe we'd catch one of them visiting someone that he wasn't supposed to be visiting. Could we catch another in a magazine store, thumbing through the wrong sort of magazine? Maybe we'd see them knocking back one too many scotches and sodas. Inevitably we'd find him or her out with their spouse or their kids, getting into one of those delightfully frank and open exchanges every spouse and every parent has gone through at the supermarket or a restaurant. And there it would all be— caught on tape!

When the fever subsided I realized how weak this revenge fantasy was. In the first place, many of these folks have security guards, chauffeurs, assistants to assistants—you probably couldn't get to them. Second, we'd never put that material on the air, because ABC has important business relationships with these people. We'd be jeopardizing tens of millions, maybe hundreds of millions of dollars with such tactics—not to mention the fact that I'd be in line for food stamps the next day.

What TV Does Right

But the real reason we wouldn't air such material is because we know these people. We know them—or at least most of them—to be good, decent people, with friends, families, and reputations. We could not imagine treating anyone we know with such contempt, without even a shred of decency. The Sermon on the Mount got it exactly right. "Do unto others."

So it doesn't help television's cause one bit that lots of people love to watch these shows. We all know that television people do not always reach for the highest shelf in the library of good taste. As one viewer put it, "I see better things and approve them; I go for the worst." Actually, it was the Roman poet Ovid who wrote that. They may watch this stuff, but I'll bet that a lot of viewers aren't very happy with themselves for watching, and they sure as hell aren't happy with us for letting them feed such appetites.

These shows undercut everything else that I and everyone else involved in television tries to say about what it is we are doing. There is so much worth praising about what is on the air today: There is so much genuinely funny comedy, moving drama, real public service, important news. I've been blessed to spend my work days first at *Sunday Morning* on CBS and now at *Nightline* on ABC, and to have been with these programs is a source of enormous satisfaction. And when you combine broadcasting with cable what we have is more choices than ever before in the history of this medium.

TV's Public Service

Nor is it required that we only talk about the most uplifting or earnest efforts. TV is a mass medium, an entertainment medium. If David Letterman's inspired foolishness makes a long day end with a smile, if Regis and Kathy Lee give viewers an hour of cotton candy in between a rushed morning and a long day, if a daytime drama gives a weary domestic worker some diversion along with a cup of coffee, that's a public service as well.

And yet after one day spent watching the parade of dysfunctional horrors, leering hosts, and audiences who were last seen crowding around the guillotine in Paris 200 years ago, I start to think about TV in the words of an old joke: "Apart from that, Mrs. Lincoln, how was the play?" Apart from the nine hours a day of human degradation and exploitation, how was today's TV?

We should not pretend to be confused about why so much of the public feels, despite all of our after-school programming and all of our community outreach programs, that we are part of the problem of a steadily coarsened public conversation and not part of the solution. Let us not pretend that we are puzzled by the misplaced sense of so many citizens that television has made us worse off, not better off.

I would finally say this to television executives: Just sit back one afternoon and turn on the television set. What you are seeing is a result of deliberate, conscious decisions of some of the most powerful, respected people in this business. This is what we choose to put out over the public airwaves. It would not be there if we did not want it to be.

PERIODICAL BIBLIOGRAPHY

The following articles have been selected to supplement the diverse views presented in this chapter. Addresses are provided for periodicals not indexed in the *Readers' Guide to Periodical Literature*, the *Alternative Press Index*, the *Social Sciences Index*, or the *Index to Legal Periodicals and Books*.

Helen Benedict	"Fear of Feminism," *Nation*, May 11, 1998.
Jane D. Brown	"Sexuality and the Mass Media: An Overview," *SIECUS Report*, April/May 1996. Available from 130 W. 42nd St., Suite 350, New York, NY 10036-7802.
Alexander Cockburn	"The War on Kids," *Nation*, June 3, 1996.
William Douglas and Beth M. Olson	"Subversion of the American Family? An Examination of Children and Parents in Television Families," *Communication Research*, February 1996.
Elizabeth L. Eisenstein	"From the Printed Word to the Moving Image," *Social Research*, Fall 1997.
Sean French	"How Would You Explain the Mysterious Tabloid World of Trash Television, Radio 1 DJs, and *Hello!* Magazine to an Inquisitive Foreigner?" *New Statesman*, April 17, 1998.
Stephen Goode	"Character and Values Confuse the Mass Media," *Insight*, March 4, 1996. Available from 3600 New York Ave. NE, Washington, DC 20002.
Katherine N. Kinnick, Dean M. Krugman, and Glen T. Cameron	"Compassion Fatigue: Communication and Burnout Toward Social Problems," *Journalism & Mass Communication Quarterly*, Fall 1996. Available from Association for Education in Journalism and Mass Communication, University of South Carolina, Le Conte College, Room 121, Columbia, SC 29208-0251.
Thomas M. Leitch	"Know-Nothing Entertainment: What to Say to Your Friends on the Right, and Why It Won't Do Any Good," *Literature-Film Quarterly*, January 1997. Available from Salisbury State University, Salisbury, MD 21801.
Joseph I. Lieberman	"Why Parents Hate TV," *Policy Review*, May/June 1996.

Martin E. Marty — "What Else Goes On," *Christian Century*, March 19, 1997.

Media Report to Women — "Media Stereotypes Noncustodial Moms: They Don't Have a Heart," Summer 1997. Available from 10606 Mantz Rd., Silver Spring, MD 20903-1247.

Michael Medved — "Children Must Be Protected from the Media's Plague of Pessimism," *USA Today*, November 1996.

Michael Parenti — "Methods of Media Manipulation," *Humanist*, July/August 1997.

Michael Rust — "Sex and Salvation: Mainstream Pop Culture Is Beginning to Reflect Changes in the Country as Baby Boomers Mature into Reflective Wonderment at What the Seventies Hath Wrought," *Insight*, December 1997.

Joe Saltzman — "Celebrity Journalism, the Public and Princess Diana," *USA Today*, January 1998.

Gloria Steinem — "What's Wrong with This Picture?" *Ms.*, March/April 1997.

David Wagner — "Making News, Breaking Ethics," *Insight*, March 1997.

IS ADVERTISING HARMFUL TO SOCIETY?

CHAPTER PREFACE

Advertising permeates modern society. Advertisements for all types of products and services can be found on billboards, magazines, televisions, newspapers, radios, subways, and buses. Increasingly, ads are becoming a staple on Internet pages as well. Many media outlets, such as television and radio stations, magazines, and newspapers, depend on the revenues generated by advertising for their survival.

Many people argue that advertising is harmful to society. Some contend that advertising promotes consumerism and materialism by suggesting—either directly or indirectly—that the acquisition of material objects such as a new car or dishwasher can provide meaning and happiness to people's lives. Critics insist that the messages of advertisers are manipulative, encouraging people to purchase products they do not really need simply to increase the profits of corporations.

On the other hand, defenders of advertising view it as a positive force that informs people about the world they live in. It can provide information about products and services at a time when the public is becoming increasingly confused by the wide array of products available, supporters argue. John E. Calfee, a resident scholar at the American Enterprise Institute, writes that advertising "routinely provides immense amounts of information that benefits primarily parties other than the advertiser." In addition, advertising is often used to promote public health and welfare, defenders insist. They point out the beneficial messages conveyed by public interest advertising campaigns that attempt to combat such social problems as teenage pregnancy, drug abuse, and smoking.

The potential positive and negative effects of advertising are debated in the following chapter.

> "Although advertising knows how to
> appeal to our deepest feelings—the
> need for security and acceptance, love
> and peace—the junk it sells us can
> provide none of these things."

ADVERTISING IS HARMFUL

Raymond A. Schroth

Defenders of advertising claim that it provides useful information about products and services. In the following viewpoint, Raymond A. Schroth presents a more critical view of advertising. Schroth contends that while advertising may seem peripheral to most people, it promotes values of materialism and consumption. The purpose of advertising, according to Schroth, is to goad people into buying products they do not need, which ultimately leaves consumers unhappy and unfulfilled. Schroth is assistant dean of Fordham College and the author of *The American Journey of Eric Sevareid*.

As you read, consider the following questions:

1. What does Schroth find offensive about an ad showing a car being lowered into a grave?
2. What does the 1954 book *People of Plenty* reveal about the role of advertising in society, according to the author?
3. What intellectual development coincided with the rise of advertising, as explained by Schroth?

Reprinted from Raymond A. Schroth, "Manic Capitalist System Fueled by Advertising," *National Catholic Reporter*, November 7, 1997, by permission of the *National Catholic Reporter*.

A cemetery. A bunch of well-off mourners all in black bunched around an open grave. Through a windshield we see a gray-faced old man with his eyes closed propped up behind the steering wheel of his car. He is a corpse, and his shiny black automobile with its dead owner in the front seat is solemnly, religiously, descending on the hydraulic lift into its grave. The widow wails hysterically, her plump face twisted in grief and tears; at the last terrible second, turning her eyes away, she extends her hand over the pit—and drops in the car keys. One mourner turns to the other and says, "She really loved that car."

The logo rolls: Infinity.

Are we offended? I guess so. It takes about 30 seconds, but behind it is an American story that we all may recognize, though it doesn't make our value system look good. A man loves his car so much he would rather be buried in it than leave it to his wife. She mourns not his loss but the lost car. It's a joke of course—a variation of the man-with-mixed-emotions joke when his mother-in-law drives his car off a cliff.

The difference is that the agency that conceived the ad doesn't just want a laugh. They presume that, at least on some level of consciousness, we will buy into the premise: An Infinity is so great that you should love it more than your spouse. So buy one. Now. Or maybe they are making fun of their clients—of us and our obsession with luxury cars. They want us to laugh at ourselves—then buy one!

THE ENGINE OF CAPITALISM

For the most part, advertising does not upset us. Which, unless the ad is political, is just their point. Indeed, it's the thesis of a brilliant documentary, *The Ad and the Ego*. The film suggests that the advertising industry has trapped us in a total social and economic environment that will limit our freedoms and destroy our planet. It was produced by the same folks who brought us *Fear and Favor in the Newsroom*, on how corporate ownership of the press controls the news flow.

Most Americans, the program suggests, see advertising as peripheral to their lives, as messages and images which they can tune in and out and then get on with the ball game or sit-com. Which is just the way the advertising industry wants it: they reach us not through the overt message—buy perfume—but through the value atmosphere they create—gorgeous-naked-Calvin-Klein-models-sure-are-pretty-and-are-having-a-terrific-time—and if I get some of that perfume, I'll be pretty too.

In short, advertising, in a capitalist country, is not just a part of the cultural or economic system—a source of information about products you might need—but is its engine, its driving force.

GOADING THE VIEWERS TO BUY

The documentary's thesis was first spelled out in historian David M. Potter's 1954 classic, *People of Plenty: Economic Abundance and the American Character*. Capitalism can thrive, Potter shows, only in an economy of abundance, where advertising's job is to get people to buy things they will never use. Advertising must goad the populace to consume, and to throw away what they buy, so they will have to buy it again. Contrary to other institutions, like the church and the university, he says, in his most devastating paragraph, "advertising has in its dynamics no motivation to seek the improvement of the individual or to impart qualities of social usefulness, unless conformity to material values can be so characterized."

COMMERCIAL MESSAGES ARE EVERYWHERE

Adcult [the "infotainment culture"] is there when we blink, it's there when we listen, it's there when we touch, it's even there to be smelled in scent strips when we open a magazine. There is barely a space in our culture not already carrying commercial messages. Look anywhere: in schools there is Channel One; in movies there is product placement; ads are in urinals, played on telephone hold, in alphanumeric displays in taxis, sent unannounced to fax machines, inside catalogs, on the video in front of the Stairmaster at the gym, on T-shirts, at the doctor's office, on grocery carts, on parking meters, on tees at golf holes, on inner-city basketball backboards, piped in along with Muzak . . . ad nauseam (and yes, even on airline vomit bags). We have to shake magazines like rag dolls to free up their pages from the "blow-in" inserts and then wrestle out the stapled- or glued-in ones before reading can begin. We now have to fast-forward through some five minutes of advertising that opens rental videotapes. President Bill Clinton's inaugural parade featured a Budweiser float. At the Smithsonian, the Orkin Pest Control Company sponsored an exhibit on exactly what it advertises it kills: insects. No venue is safe. Is there a blockbuster museum show not decorated with corporate logos? The Public Broadcasting Service is littered with "underwriting announcements" that look and sound almost exactly like what PBS claims they are not: commercials.

James B. Twitchell, *Current*, December 1996.

For this anti-advertising video, California Newsreel has brought together seven scholarly talking heads from the United States and Canada. Most have written books, produced videos, testified before Congress, and, as far as I can tell, have had—to my regret—limited impact on public policy.

As they talk, we see: Beautiful women soap up their bodies in the shower and pull down their shorts to reveal their tight-bathing-suited behinds; good-looking guys romp in the surf and hug the giddy girls who greet them on the beach; chubby suburbanites slave over hot dogs on a grill; a naked model, clutching her breasts, strolls through a pub under the ogling eyes of beer guzzlers. Calvin Klein reminds us that the human body is good and beautiful.

CREATING A CONSUMER SOCIETY

If you want a microcosm of the values of the advertising industry, try The New Improved Times Square—no longer all porn and prostitutes but a Hell's Kitchen version of Disneyworld, a blazing maze of costly schlock, which may not be sexual porn but a level of gluttonous consumerism not much better.

Here are a few themes from *The Ad and the Ego*.

• The rise of advertising coincided with a change in the way we viewed human nature. Prior to World War I, we saw humans primarily as rational beings. In the 1920s, under the influence of Sigmund Freud and Ivan Pavlov, we began to see one another as irrational creatures of instinct, controlled by unconscious desires, and, like Pavlov's dog (who barks all during the film), responsive to whatever stimuli to which we can be conditioned. This coincided, in popular culture, with the triumph of the image over the word. Thus the way to capture a mind is to present symbols that tap the emotions—the levels of the unconscious that make viewers feel insecure and in need of whatever advertisers can sell.

• Advertisers create and exploit these insecurities. Life is a competition to be noticed. No one will like me if I have dry, flaky skin, if my teeth don't glisten—if I don't have a "clean mouth taste for hours." No one will hug me if I sweat. If I'm a creaky old grandpa and don't take Motrin, Aleve, and Advil, and I can't play touch football with 12-year-olds, my grandchildren will put me on the shelf. If I go to the office party with a woman who is not a young woman who looks like the ones on TV, I might as well forget about my future at my company.

• By creating a maximum consumption society, advertising fosters attitudes that will ruin the planet. The Third World must exist solely to meet the needs of the First (us). In America, there is now one car for every person. To achieve the same ratio in the Third World, the auto/advertising industry must sell millions of gas guzzlers to, for example, China, where that many cars will ruin their environment. I have seen this Bangkok, now a "prosperous," polluted, clogged snarl of highways and gridlock. The film's prime example of this attitude is the Gulf War, where, to maintain "our way of life" (cheap oil), George Bush didn't care how many Iraqis he had to kill and the Pentagon censored the news so we could not see the consequences of our policy.

LEARNING TO LIVE WITH LESS

One of my Fordham students, Courtney Shannon, had it right in her reflection paper on Henry David Thoreau: "Consumers have too many choices. There are hundreds of different brands of clothes, yet each brand does the same function of keeping a person covered. A Lexus and a Toyota are both modes of transportation, yet there is a price difference of over $40,000 between the two cars. The simplicity of life has been lost. Crime is the consumer's partner. It is becoming nearly impossible to separate the two. The rich flaunt what they own. The poor demoralize themselves to get the material goods that will make them appear richer than they are."

What do the *The Ad and the Ego* narrators not tell us? That the advertising industry has some of the most talented men and women in the communications industry and that the ads are often better, in both technique and entertainment value, than the TV shows. Nor do they allow ad creators to speak for themselves. In short, the documentary itself is an ad and, like all ads, propaganda. "Good" propaganda perhaps, but propaganda nevertheless.

Furthermore, its proposed solution—to develop alternative means of communication that don't have to be financed by advertising—is pretty fuzzy. Cable stations are already being gobbled up by networks, and the Internet has quickly become a glut of commercials smothering tidbits of real news.

The great strength of *The Ad and the Ego* is the spirituality of its message. We must learn to live with less, it argues, to see that mere consumption does not make us happy. The curriculum guide asks students to list the products in their attics, closets, and garages they no longer use. To realize that although advertising knows how to appeal to our deepest feelings—the need for security and acceptance, love and peace—the junk it sells us can provide none of these things. Indeed, it can only aggravate the problem, keep us unsatisfied and goad us to stuff up again on painkillers, sexy perfumes, junk foods and fast cars that will rush us to our graves.

"People find advertising very useful indeed."

ADVERTISING IS NOT HARMFUL

John E. Calfee

Advertising is often blamed for manipulating people and persuading them to buy products they neither want nor need. In the following viewpoint, John E. Calfee argues that, contrary to the claims of critics, advertising is beneficial to consumers in a number of ways. For example, according to Calfee, advertisements provide the public with information about health issues and about new treatments for medical problems. In addition, he states, competition among advertisers often leads them to reveal harmful information about their products or to lower their prices. Calfee is a resident scholar at the American Enterprise Institute, a conservative think tank in Washington, D.C., and the author of *Fear of Persuasion: A New Perspective on Advertising and Regulation*.

As you read, consider the following questions:

1. According to the author, how did the Kellogg Corporation work with the National Cancer Institute to inform consumers about the health benefits of a high-fiber diet?
2. What are the benefits of "less-bad" advertising, in Calfee's opinion?
3. How did less-bad advertising affect cigarette sales in the 1950s, as reported by the author?

Excerpted from John E. Calfee, "How Advertising Informs to Our Benefit," *Consumers' Research Magazine*, April 1998. Reprinted with permission.

A great truth about advertising is that it is a tool for communicating information and shaping markets. It is one of the forces that compel sellers to cater to the desires of consumers. Almost everyone knows this because consumers use advertising every day, and they miss advertising when they cannot get it. This fact does not keep politicians and opinion leaders from routinely dismissing the value of advertising. But the truth is that people find advertising very useful indeed.

Of course, advertising primarily seeks to persuade and everyone knows this, too. The typical ad tries to induce a consumer to do one particular thing—usually, buy a product—instead of a thousand other things. There is nothing obscure about this purpose or what it means for buyers. Decades of data and centuries of intuition reveal that all consumers everywhere are deeply suspicious of what advertisers say and why they say it. This skepticism is in fact the driving force that makes advertising so effective. The persuasive purpose of advertising and the skepticism with which it is met are two sides of a single process. Persuasion and skepticism work in tandem so advertising can do its job in competitive markets. Hence, ads represent the seller's self interest, consumers know this, and sellers know that consumers know it.

By understanding this process more fully, we can sort out much of the popular confusion surrounding advertising and how it benefits consumers.

How Useful Is Advertising?

Just how useful is the connection between advertising and information? At first blush, the process sounds rather limited. Volvo ads tell consumers that Volvos have side-impact air bags, people learn a little about the importance of air bags, and Volvo sells a few more cars. This seems to help hardly anyone except Volvo and its customers.

But advertising does much more. It routinely provides immense amounts of information that benefits primarily parties other than the advertiser. This may sound odd, but it is a logical result of market forces and the nature of information itself.

The ability to use information to sell products is an incentive to create new information through research. Whether the topic is nutrition, safety, or more mundane matters like how to measure amplifier power, the necessity of achieving credibility with consumers and critics requires much of this research to be placed in the public domain, and that it rest upon some academic credentials. That kind of research typically produces results that apply to more than just the brands sold by the firm sponsoring the research. The lack of property rights to such "pure" information ensures that this extra information is available at no charge. Both consumers and competitors may borrow the new information for their own purposes.

Advertising also elicits additional information from other sources. Claims that are striking, original, forceful or even merely obnoxious will generate news stories about the claims, the controversies they cause, the reactions of competitors (A price war? A splurge of comparison ads?), the reactions of consumers and the remarks of governments and independent authorities.

Probably the most concrete, pervasive, and persistent example of competitive advertising that works for the public good is price advertising. Its effect is invariably to heighten competition and reduce prices, even the prices of firms that assiduously avoid mentioning prices in their own advertising.

There is another area where the public benefits of advertising are less obvious but equally important. The unremitting nature of consumer interest in health, and the eagerness of sellers to cater to consumer desires, guarantee that advertising related to health will provide a storehouse of telling observations on the ways in which the benefits of advertising extend beyond the interests of advertisers to include the interests of the public at large.

A CASCADE OF INFORMATION

Here is probably the best documented example of why advertising is necessary for consumer welfare. In the 1970s, public health experts described compelling evidence that people who eat more fiber are less likely to get cancer, especially cancer of the colon, which happens to be the second leading cause of deaths from cancer in the United States. By 1979, the U.S. Surgeon General was recommending that people eat more fiber in order to prevent cancer.

Consumers appeared to take little notice of these recommendations, however. The National Cancer Institute decided that more action was needed. NCI's cancer prevention division undertook to communicate the new information about fiber and cancer to the general public. Their goal was to change consumer diets and reduce the risk of cancer, but they had little hope of success given the tiny advertising budgets of federal agencies like NCI.

Their prospects unexpectedly brightened in 1984. NCI received a call from the Kellogg Corporation, whose All-Bran cereal held a commanding market share of the high-fiber segment. Kellogg proposed to use All-Bran advertising as a vehicle for NCI's public service messages. NCI thought that was an excellent idea. Soon, an agreement was reached in which NCI would review Kellogg's ads and labels for accuracy and value before Kellogg began running their fiber-cancer ads.

WHAT ADVERTISING DOES

• Provides information about products and services—what a product does and what kind of performance and benefits can be expected. For example, an anti-histamine for allergies that doesn't cause drowsiness.

• Introduces consumers to new products and new uses for old products, so that consumers have more choices at varying quality levels and prices. The superior or more economical product that no one knows about will benefit few consumers.

• Compares attributes of one product with another similar one (often on objectively measurable attributes or price), so that consumers can learn about a product that is more attractive or suitable for them.

Frances B. Smith, *Consumer's Research Magazine*, April 1997.

The new Kellogg All-Bran campaign opened in October 1984. A typical ad began with the headline, "At last some news about cancer you can live with." The ad continued: "The National Cancer Institute believes a high fiber, low fat diet may reduce your risk of some kinds of cancer. The National Cancer Institute reports some very good health news. There is growing evidence that may link a high fiber, low fat diet to lower incidence of some kinds of cancer. That's why one of their strongest recommendations is to eat high-fiber foods. If you compare, you'll find Kellogg's All-Bran has nine grams of fiber per serving. No other cereal has more. So start your day with a bowl of Kellogg's All-Bran or mix it with your regular cereal."

The campaign quickly achieved two things. One was to create a regulatory crisis between two agencies. The Food and Drug Administration thought that if a food was advertised as a way to prevent cancer, it was being marketed as a drug. Then the FDA's regulations for drug labeling would kick in. The food would be reclassified as a drug and would be removed from the market until the seller either stopped making the health claims or put the product through the clinical testing necessary to obtain formal approval as a drug.

But food advertising is regulated by the Federal Trade Commission, not the FDA. The FTC thought Kellogg's ads were nondeceptive and were therefore perfectly legal. In fact, it thought the ads should be encouraged. The Director of the FTC's Bureau of Consumer Protection declared that "the [Kellogg] ad has presented important public health recommendations in an accurate, useful, and substantiated way. It informs the members of the public that there is a body of data suggesting certain relationships between cancer and diet that they may find important." The FTC won this political battle, and the ads continued.

The second instant effect of the All-Bran campaign was to unleash a flood of health claims. Vegetable oil manufacturers advertised that cholesterol was associated with coronary heart disease, and that vegetable oil does not contain cholesterol. Margarine ads did the same, and added that vitamin A is essential for good vision. Ads for calcium products (such as certain antacids) provided vivid demonstrations of the effects of osteoporosis (which weakens bones in old age), and recounted the advice of experts to increase dietary calcium as a way to prevent osteoporosis. Kellogg's competitors joined in citing the National Cancer Institute dietary recommendations.

Nor did things stop there. In the face of consumer demand for better and fuller information, health claims quickly evolved from a blunt tool to a surprisingly refined mechanism. Cereals were advertised as high in fiber and low in sugar or fat or sodium. Ads for an upscale brand of bread noted: "Well, most high-fiber bran cereals may be high in fiber, but often only one kind: insoluble. It's this kind of fiber that helps promote regularity. But there's also a kind of fiber known as soluble, which most high-fiber bran cereals have in very small amounts, if at all. Yet diets high in this kind of fiber may actually lower your serum cholesterol, a risk factor for some heart diseases." Cereal boxes became convenient sources for a summary of what made for a good diet. . . .

"LESS-BAD" ADVERTISING

There is a troubling possibility, however. Is it not possible that in their selective and carefully calculated use of outside information, advertisers have the power to focus consumer attention exclusively on the positive, i.e., on what is good about the brand or even the entire product class? Won't automobile ads talk up style, comfort, and extra safety, while food ads do taste and convenience, cigarette ads do flavor and lifestyle, and airlines do comfort and frequency of departure, all the while leaving consumers to search through other sources to find all the things that are wrong with products?

In fact, this is not at all what happens. Here is why: Everything for sale has something wrong with it, if only the fact that you have to pay for it. Some products, of course, are notable for their faults. The most obvious examples involve tobacco and health, but there are also food and heart disease, drugs and side effects, vacations and bad weather, automobiles and accidents, airlines and delay, among others.

Products and their problems bring into play one of the most important ways in which the competitive market induces sellers to serve the interests of buyers. No matter what the product, there are usually a few brands that are "less bad" than the others. The natural impulse is to advertise that advantage—"less cholesterol," "less fat," "less dangerous," and so on. Such provocative claims tend to have an immediate impact. The targets often retaliate; maybe their brands are less bad in a different respect (less salt?). The ensuing struggle brings better information, more informed choices, and improved products.

Perhaps the most riveting episode of "less-bad" advertising ever seen occurred, amazingly enough, in the industry that most people assume is the master of avoiding saying anything bad about its product.

"LESS-BAD" CIGARETTE ADS

Cigarette advertising was once very different from what it is today. Cigarettes first became popular around the time of World War I, and they came to dominate the tobacco market in the 1920s. Steady and often dramatic sales increases continued into the 1950s, always with vigorous support from advertising. Tobacco advertising was duly celebrated as an outstanding example of the power and creativity of advertising. Yet amazingly, much of the advertising focused on what was wrong with smoking, rather than what people liked about smoking.

The very first ad for the very first mass-marketed American cigarette brand (Camel, the same brand recently under attack for its use of a cartoon character) said, "Camel Cigarettes will not sting the tongue and will not parch the throat." When Old Gold broke into the market in the mid-1920s, it did so with an ad campaign about coughs and throats and harsh cigarette smoke. It settled on the slogan, "Not a cough in a carload."

Competitors responded in kind. Soon, advertising left no doubt about what was wrong with smoking. Lucky Strike ads said, "No Throat Irritation—No Cough . . . we . . . removed . . . harmful corrosive acids," and later on, "Do you inhale? What's there to be afraid of? . . . famous purifying process removes certain impurities." Camel's famous tag line, "more doctors smoke

Camels than any other brand," carried a punch precisely because many authorities thought smoking was unhealthy (cigarettes were called "coffin nails" back then), and smokers were eager for reassurance in the form of smoking by doctors themselves. This particular ad, which was based on surveys of physicians, ran in one form or another from 1933 to 1955. It achieved prominence partly because physicians practically never endorsed non-therapeutic products.

Things really got interesting in the early 1950s, when the first persuasive medical reports on smoking and lung cancer reached the public. These reports created a phenomenal stir among smokers and the public generally. People who do not understand how advertising works would probably assume that cigarette manufacturers used advertising to divert attention away from the cancer reports. In fact, they did the opposite.

Small brands could not resist the temptation to use advertising to scare smokers into switching brands. They inaugurated several spectacular years of "fear advertising" that sought to gain competitive advantage by exploiting smokers' new fear of cancer. Lorillard, the beleaguered seller of Old Gold, introduced Kent, a new filter brand supported by ad claims like these: "Sensitive smokers get real health protection with new Kent," "Do you love a good smoke but not what the smoke does to you?" and "Takes out more nicotine and tars than any other leading cigarette—the difference in protection is priceless," illustrated by television ads showing the black tar trapped by Kent's filters.

Other manufacturers came out with their own filter brands, and raised the stakes with claims like, "Nose, throat, and accessory organs not adversely affected by smoking Chesterfields. First such report ever published about any cigarette," "Takes the fear out of smoking," and "Stop worrying . . . Philip Morris and only Philip Morris is entirely free of irritation used [sic] in all other leading cigarettes."

These ads threatened to demolish the industry. Cigarette sales plummeted by 3% in 1953 and a remarkable 6% in 1954. Never again, not even in the face of the most impassioned antismoking publicity by the Surgeon General or the FDA, would cigarette consumption decline as rapidly as it did during these years of entirely market-driven antismoking ad claims by the cigarette industry itself. . . .

The Benefits of Price Advertising

Less-bad can be found wherever competitive advertising is allowed. I already described the health-claims-for-foods saga, which featured fat and cholesterol and the dangers of cancer and heart disease. Price advertising is another example. Prices are the most stubbornly negative product feature of all, because they represent the simple fact that the buyer must give up something else. There is no riper target for comparative advertising. When sellers advertise lower prices, competitors reduce their prices and advertise that, and soon a price war is in the works. This process so strongly favors consumers over the industry that one of the first things competitors do when they form a trade group is to propose an agreement to restrict or ban price advertising (if not ban all advertising). When that fails, they try to get advertising regulators to stop price ads, an attempt that unfortunately often succeeds.

Someone is always trying to scare customers into switching brands out of fear of the product itself. The usual effect is to impress upon consumers what they do not like about the product. In 1991, when Americans were worried about insurance companies going broke, a few insurance firms advertised that they were more solvent than their competitors. In May 1997, United Airlines began a new ad campaign that started out by reminding fliers of all the inconveniences that seem to crop up during air travel.

Health information is a fixture in "less-bad" advertising. Ads for sleeping aids sometimes focus on the issue of whether they are habit-forming. In March 1996, a medical journal reported that the pain reliever acetaminophen, the active ingredient in Tylenol, can cause liver damage in heavy drinkers. This fact immediately became the focus of ads for Advil, a competing product. A public debate ensued, conducted through advertising, talk shows, news reports and pronouncements from medical authorities. The result: consumers learned a lot more than they had known before about the fact that all drugs have side effects. The press noted that this dispute may have helped consumers, but it hurt the pain reliever industry. Similar examples abound.

We have, then, a general rule: sellers will use comparative advertising when permitted to do so, even if it means spreading bad information about a product instead of favorable information. The mechanism usually takes the form of less-bad claims. One can hardly imagine a strategy more likely to give consumers the upper hand in the give and take of the marketplace. Less-bad claims are a primary means by which advertising serves markets and consumers rather than sellers. They completely refute the naive idea that competitive advertising will emphasize only the sellers' virtues while obscuring their problems.

"The tobacco industry made its
money by marketing cigarettes to
children, knowing full well that
cigarettes are addictive projects with
severe health consequences."

REGULATING TOBACCO ADS PROTECTS CHILDREN

Jack Reed

In the following viewpoint Senator Jack Reed argues in support of the "Children's Health Preservation and Tobacco Advertising Compliance Act," introduced to the U.S. Senate on March 13, 1998. This act would prevent tobacco companies from getting tax deductions from advertising directed at children. According to Reed, tobacco companies currently enjoy a large tax deduction for advertising. This bill would not eliminate the deduction unless tobacco companies targeted their advertising at children. Reed believes that tobacco companies have always targeted youths and that only tough legislation can prevent the companies from continuing to target them in the future. The bill was referred to the Senate Committee on Finance for possible inclusion in a comprehensive tobacco bill. Jack Reed is a Democratic senator from Rhode Island.

As you read, consider the following questions:

1. According to the author, how much money do children spend on tobacco products each year?
2. How much did tobacco companies spend on advertising in 1995, according to Reed?
3. What evidence does the author present to suggest that the Joe Camel ads were effective in reaching children?

Excerpted from Jack Reed's testimony before the U.S. Senate regarding the Children's Health Preservation and Tobacco Advertising Compliance Act, 105th Cong., 1st sess., March 12, 1998.

M r. President, I rise today to announce legislation that would amend the Internal Revenue Code to deny tobacco companies any tax deduction for their advertising and promotional expenses, when those ads are aimed at America's most impressionable group, children.

This bill addresses a key element in our ongoing public debate on tobacco: industry's ceaseless efforts to market to children. My legislation can stand on its own, or can easily be incorporated into a comprehensive tobacco bill. With or without Congressional action on the state attorney generals' tobacco settlement, it is time for Congress to put a stop to the tobacco industry's practice of luring children into untimely disease and death.

I am pleased to be joined today in introducing this legislation with Senators [Barbara] Boxer and [John] Chafee, and I would also like to recognize the leadership of my colleagues on this issue. Senator [Tom] Harkin, along with former Senator [Bill] Bradley and others, has made continuous efforts over the years to completely eliminate the tax deduction for tobacco advertising. And while I concur with Senator Harkin that the deduction is a questionable use of our tax dollars, I would like to emphasize to my colleagues that this bill does not eliminate the deduction for tobacco manufacturers, as long as they do not advertise to children.

Limiting the promotion of tobacco products to children is a necessary part of any comprehensive effort to prevent tobacco use by minors. My legislation offers a constitutionally sound way to enforce strong tobacco advertising restrictions, with or without federal tobacco legislation on the proposed tobacco settlement.

The advertising restrictions contained in our bill are included in S.1638, legislation introduced by Senator [Kent] Conrad, cosponsored by myself and 29 other Senators. S.1638 establishes strong restrictions regarding the promotion of tobacco products to minors.

Under my bill, if tobacco manufacturers do not comply with the proposed advertising restrictions, the manufacturer's ability to deduct the cost of tobacco advertising and promotion expenses would be disallowed.

These advertising restrictions are appropriately tailored to prevent the advertising and marketing of tobacco to minors. The restrictions contained in this legislation are similar to those contained in the FDA [Food and Drug Administration] rule and the June 20 proposed settlement. Key components of these restrictions include: a prohibition on point of sale advertising except in adult only stores and tobacco outlets; a ban on outdoor advertising within 1000 feet of schools and publicly-owned playgrounds, and outdoor advertising beyond those areas restricted to black-and-white text only; and, a prohibition on brand-name sponsorship of sporting or entertainment events.

On numerous occasions, tobacco industry executives have indicated that unless they receive liability protections, they will continue to advertise as they do now. Today I am offering an alternative enforcement mechanism because failure to act on this issue is a failure to meet the needs of our children.

YOUTH SMOKING

Mr. President, the importance of this issue is enormous. The facts speak for themselves. Today, some 50 million Americans are addicted to tobacco. One of every three long-term users of tobacco will die from a disease related to their tobacco use. About three-fourths (70 percent) of smokers want to quit, but less than one-quarter are successful in doing so.

Tobacco addiction is clearly a problem that starts with children: almost 90 percent of adult smokers started using tobacco at or before age 18. The average youth smoker begins at age 13 and becomes a daily smoker by age 14½.

Each year, one million children become regular smokers—and one-third of them will die prematurely of lung cancer, emphysema, and similar tobacco caused diseases. Unless current trends are reversed, five million kids under 18 currently alive today will die from tobacco related disease.

In my home state of Rhode Island, while overall cigarette use is declining slightly, it has increased by more than 25 percent among high-schoolers.

It is far too easy for children to buy cigarettes and chewing tobacco through vending machines and at retail outlets. Despite the fact that it is against the law in all 50 states to sell cigarettes and smokeless tobacco to minors, children purchase an estimated $1.26 billion worth of tobacco products each year.

THE INDUSTRY'S TRACK RECORD

As we look to a bright future for our children, Congress must learn from the lessons of the past. Those lessons teach us that the tobacco industry made its money by marketing cigarettes to children, knowing full well that cigarettes are addictive products with severe health consequences. The proposed settlement reached last June is based on the presumption that this industry can and wants to change its corporate culture—a culture that has yielded incredible revenue by capitalizing on the vulnerabilities of our children.

The story of the tobacco industry and youth smoking in the United States is the story of the advertising industry. In the 1920s, cigarette manufacturers solicited doctors to try their products, later advertising '20,679 Physicians Say Luckies are Less Irritating' and 'For Digestion's sake, smoke Camels.' In a case against Reynolds Tobacco, decided in March 1950, the FTC found that Camel advertisements had been worded in such a way as to declare that the brand was harmless, and, as such, were false and deceptive.

PROMOTING TOBACCO TO UNDERAGE SMOKERS

Despite industry claims that its advertisements and promotions do not target youth specifically, tobacco marketing reaches and influences a substantial number of underage persons. Children are exposed to widespread tobacco advertising, even at an early age. The Joe Camel campaign attracted the attention of children younger than 13 years more effectively than any other age group, including adults. Similarly, promotional activities, which include widespread catalog and specialty item distribution (eg, free to-bacco samples, lighters, apparel), reach large numbers of under-age smokers and potential smokers. In a survey of 1125 teenagers nationwide, about half had received promotional items.

Laurence O. Gostin et al., *JAMA*, February 5, 1997.

An advertisement in 1953 read: 'This is it. L&M filters are just what the doctor ordered.' Another advertisement from that time period claimed: 'More Doctors smoke Camels than any other cigarette.'

And today, we have Winston ads that attempt to sound like a health food promotion, proclaiming 'no additives.' The new Camel ad—'Live Out Loud'—is a not so subtle stand in for the 'cool' Joe Camel. . . .

From recently released documents, we know that the tobacco industry has sought to market its tobacco products to children for decades. News reports disclosed that an RJR researcher named Claude Teague had written a 1973 memo that stated 'if our Company is to survive and prosper, over the long-term we must get our share of the youth market.'

Documents obtained through the Mangini litigation further document these efforts. A Presentation from CA Tucker, Vice President of Marketing, to the Board of Directors of RJR Indus-tries (Sept. 30, 1974) concluded: 'this young adult market, the 14-24 age group . . . represent(s) tomorrow's cigarette business.' That same presentation said: 'For Salem, significant improvements have been made in the advertising, designed for more youth adult appeal under its greenery/refreshment theme. These include: more true-to-life young adult situations. More dominant visuals. A greater spirit of fun . . . For Camel Filter, we . . . will have pinpointed efforts against young adults through its sponsorship of sports car racing and motorcycling.' The Mangini documents also demonstrate that RJR has been secretly conducting extensive surveys of the smoking habits of teenagers for decades.

Given this track record, I am deeply skeptical of the tobacco industry and its willingness to change its behavior. Yet they say they are willing—my bill will put them to the test.

BILLIONS SPENT EACH YEAR ON TOBACCO ADVERTISING

At every turn, the tobacco industry has come up with a slick new way to hook kids on tobacco. And we know from research that advertising targeted to children can play a pivotal role in an adolescent's decision to smoke.

Through the years, the tobacco companies have designed a way to attract generation after generation to smoking. Examples of industry practices are endless. Eighty-six percent of underage smokers prefer one of the three most heavily advertised brands— Marlboro, Newport or Camel.

One of the advertising campaigns most markedly aimed at young people is the Joe Camel campaign. After RJ Reynolds introduced this campaign, Camel's market share among underage smokers jumped from 3 percent to over 13 percent in 3 years.

Although Congress banned cigarette advertising on television in 1970, tobacco companies routinely circumvent this restriction through the sponsorship of sporting events that gives their products exposure through television.

Data from the Federal Trade Commission indicates how much the industry spends on these activities. Advertising and promotion expenditures have increased tenfold since 1975. In 1975, the industry spent $491 million. In 1995 alone, tobacco manufacturers spent $4.9 billion on advertising and promotional expenditures.

The federal government subsidizes tobacco advertising through a tax deduction (generally a 35 percent deduction) for advertising expenses. In 1995, this subsidy cost the American taxpayers approximately $1.6 billion. In terms of lost revenues to the Federal Treasury, it is certainly not an insignificant amount of money.

In effect, the federal government is subsidizing the industry's advertising costs. For example, in 1995, the cost of the cigarette advertising deduction covered the total amount spent by the industry on coupons, multi-pak promotions, and retail value added items, such as key chains, and point of sale advertising —the kind of items that are most attractive to our children.

CONSTITUTIONAL ISSUES

The First Amendment does not entitle tobacco companies to target children. The Supreme Court has said that commercial speech enjoys only limited protection. It is interesting to note that tobacco companies have not challenged the right of the government to restrict their advertising in other ways, such as the 1971 ban on broadcast advertising for tobacco products.

The industry has said that it must be offered liability limits for them to 'consent' to advertising restrictions. In effect, the industry is saying, if Congress wants the companies to stop illegal efforts to induce children to smoke, then Congress should protect the industry from legal action. And the hypocrisy of the industry's position is that they would like the immunity protections in statute but say that the advertising restrictions 'cannot be imposed by statute or by rule.'

Some in the industry have suggested that without liability protections, the tobacco industry will continue to market to children. A *USA Today* article on February 19, 1998, stated that industry spokesman Meyer Koplow 'warned that the industry might return to practices such as cartoon advertising if Congress fails to grant protection from lawsuits.'

The tobacco industry, the advertising industry, and others have said that they would challenge statutory restrictions on advertising. While I believe that S.1368 and other proposals do not violate the Constitution, I recognize the uncertainty surrounding the provisions in this and other bills.

What is certain is that Congress has the authority over the tax code. This legislation uses that authority to put an end to the tobacco industry's practice of targeting children.

Mr. President, I urge my colleagues to join me in this effort to protect America's children.

| "Almost all studies of children ...
show that cigarette advertising
affects brand loyalty but does not
induce smoking."

TOBACCO ADVERTISING SHOULD
NOT BE REGULATED

John Berlau

In the following viewpoint, John Berlau argues that regulations
on tobacco advertising are unnecessary and counterproductive.
Advertising does not compel people to smoke, he maintains, so
regulations will not reduce the number of new smokers. According to Berlau, the increase in teen smoking in recent years
has not been caused by advertising but by the same factors that
have led to an increase in illegal drug use. Berlau believes that
regulations actually benefit tobacco companies because they
serve to limit competition between brands. Berlau was formerly
a political analyst at Consumer Alert and is currently a regular
contributor to Insight, a weekly newsmagazine.

As you read, consider the following questions:

1. Why does the author believe state and federal government
   agencies are being hypocritical in their attacks on tobacco
   companies?
2. Why did tobacco industries favor legislation that required
   them to place the surgeon general's warning on their
   products, according to Elizabeth Whelan, as quoted by
   Berlau?
3. What evidence does the author give to support his assertion
   that tobacco personalities like Joe Camel have little to do with
   whether or not children smoke?

S tates' attorneys general and the White House are fighting tobacco giants over Americans' health risks from smoking. But
the same bunch—and other crusaders—stand aside while other
government agencies and politicians promote the industry and
make billions of dollars from it. Is there an end in sight to this
brand of hypocrisy?

As lawsuits rage through state courts, state attorneys general
posture as defenders of good health and clean air, and highly-
paid executives of big tobacco companies are portrayed as male-
factors of great wealth, it becomes clear to even the merest tyro
that there is a vast hypocrisy at work on the issue of tobacco.
Many a Washington bureaucrat and political boss is thankful that
it's not laser lights but kliegs that are focusing on this smokey issue. That's because behind the haze created by the public-policy
squabbling about tobacco are political games as slick as that of
New York's finest card sharps who attract the suckers with "now
you see 'em, now you don't!"

Consider for example the Food and Drug Administration, or
FDA, and its new authority to regulate tobacco giants as purveyors of medical devices containing the drug nicotine. At the same
time that the FDA is crusading effectively to control the products of the tobacco industry, virtually across the street is the U.S.
Department of Agriculture, or USDA, actively working to promote, sell, subsidize and propagate the same commodity in the
United States and overseas. A few blocks on either side of Washington's Independence Avenue are the Congress and executive
agencies that levy and collect millions of dollars in taxes and
contributions from the politically incorrect target industry.

LEADING TO A SLIPPERY SLOPE

So what's going on?

There's a leveling-off after a mostly steady 30-year decline in
smoking rates, and people who oppose smoking by harassing
others are wondering if there may be a backlash against neo-
puritanical elements of their movement as there has been to the
notion that big government ought to tell customers of the tobacco industry what they can put in their mouths. Many also
wonder if the demonizing of cigarettes will lead to a "slippery
slope" in which caffeine, fatty food, chocolate and anything else
the public-health community might deem bad or politically incorrect becomes subject to regulation or prohibition.

Such questions arise not only because of shifting social concerns often targeted by fringe elements, or hard-to-believe "evidence" from both sides that tobacco will or will not turn us into

a pillar of salt. They also arise because of the contradictory and conflicting nature of the government's public crusade to bash cigarette makers at the same time it is giving hefty support to the tobacco business in other ways. The tobacco support program, for example. Although the Congress revised the program in the eighties to run at "no net cost" to the government, the Congressional Budget Office reports that the program still "can have substantial outlays in a given year—1994 outlays were $693 million—but if the program functions as intended, it should have no net cost to the government over time." Perhaps so, but this does not include millions of dollars spent annually in administration costs at the USDA and other federal and state agencies actively working on behalf of the tobacco industry.

Then there are the costs of federal and state-sponsored promotions of tobacco sales overseas. Beyond support for American firms to sell, ship and blend tobacco products for export, there's also support for foreign buyers of the USA-grown leaf, which is stored, sold and advertised aggressively abroad with the help of the federal government. The Departments of State, Commerce and Defense push USA tobacco overseas in bilateral, unilateral and other forms of diplomatic overtures that include tobacco imports.

NEGOTIATING A CEASE-FIRE

For the moment, tobacco companies are negotiating a cease-fire with legislators, state prosecutors, and some antismoking groups such as the Campaign for Tobacco-Free Kids. They are trying to settle with trial lawyers representing smokers and their families and states' attorneys general suing for Medicaid reimbursements on the health costs of smoking-related diseases. Senate Majority Leader Trent Lott of Mississippi told the Bloomberg News wire service that, if a settlement is agreed to, "it will have a lot of momentum," and likely a blessing will sail through Congress.

Bloomberg also quoted a lawyer involved in the talks who said that "80 percent of the deal is done." Reports from the talks indicate that the deal on the table would have the tobacco companies pay $300 billion to the states, trial attorneys, and smokers and their families. The companies also would agree to bans on billboards and the use of humans and cartoon characters such as Joe Camel in advertising, and possibly to acceptance of more FDA regulation, although the companies are currently challenging the agency's authority to regulate them. In exchange, they would get limitations on their horrendous civil liability. [The settlement fell through in the spring of 1998. However, R.J. Reynolds has agreed to discontinue the Joe Camel campaign.]

Why would tobacco companies agree to such sweeping regulation? Longtime antitobacco crusader Elizabeth Whelan, who derides the proposed settlement as a "drug payoff," gives this explanation: "The only thing they want is immunity from private lawsuits."

Whelan, founder and president of the New York–based American Council on Science and Health and author of *A Smoking Gun: How the Tobacco Industry Gets Away with Murder*, points out that tobacco companies have managed historically to benefit from regulation and in fact asked the Congress for many of the regulations about which they complain. Whelan calls the surgeon general's warning, which Congress required on cigarette packaging and in ads shortly after the government declared smoking hazardous, to be "the biggest prize of all" for tobacco companies. "It had nothing to do with the surgeon general," Whelan said. "It was put on there by Philip Morris. They wrote the legislation, and it gave them immunity from [most] lawsuits. It gave them a special status."

ADVERTISING AND COMPETITION

Similarly, the cigarette companies led the charge for the television and radio advertising ban that Congress passed in 1970 after the FCC required broadcasters to give response time to tobacco opponents. Smoking rates, which had been declining dramatically, actually increased in the first few years after the ad ban went into effect. Walter Olson, a senior fellow at New York's conservative Manhattan Institute who analyzes legal and economic issues, says the cigarette companies will probably agree to advertising restrictions in the current settlements as "a classic Br'er Rabbit ploy." Olson says that the tobacco companies "would be delighted to be thrown into that briar patch" because it would save them money and protect the major brands from competition.

"Advertising is an enormous expense, and the evidence is that it does very little to boost short-term demand for the product," Olson points out. "To prevent people from being tempted by new brands [of cigarettes], all the existing brands advertise heavily. Take away the right to advertise, it becomes almost impossible to launch a new brand. Everyone stops having to worry as much about incursions on their market share, and at the same time they have just saved one of their largest dollar items of expenditure. You can predict very reliably that if you ban advertising and change nothing else about the system, you will increase tobacco company profits for many years to come."

True, you would get rid of the infamous Joe Camel, the favorite whipping mammal of the antismoking movement. But George Washington University public-policy professor Howard Beales, the former deputy director of the Bureau of Consumer Protection of the Federal Commission, which regulates cigarette advertising, says that Joe and other tobacco personalities don't have much to do with whether kids smoke. "Given that they smoke, advertising may have an effect on what brand they smoke, but the much more important question is whether it has an effect on smoking," Beales says. Studying a California survey of 5,000 teens, Beales found that advertising "did not have any significant relationship to teen smoking." He says the increase in teen smoking, which has risen 7 percent in the past 5 years, is probably related to the simultaneous increase in teen drug use. And that definitely cannot be explained by advertising since advertising narcotics is illegal.

Beales says that almost all studies of children and adults show that cigarette advertising affects brand loyalty but does not induce smoking. However, in the early fifties, unrestricted cigarette advertising may have been partly responsible for decreasing cigarette use. In a 1986 article in *Regulation* magazine entitled "The Ghost of Cigarette Advertising Past," FTC economist John Calfee pointed out that when studies first came out in the early fifties linking cigarette smoking to cancer, new companies like Philip Morris developed filtered cigarettes and advertised that their brands took "the fear out of smoking."

Calfee argues that the side effect of this "fear advertising" was to "remind consumers constantly of the worrisome symptoms associated with smoking." Tobacco growers and dominant firms such as R.J. Reynolds were furious because, as the new companies got a higher market share, per-capita cigarette consumption declined 9 percent over two years, the largest drop to this day. However, cigarette consumption went right back up after the FTC issued regulations banning health claims in advertisements because, the agency said, the dangers hadn't been proved.

Calfee, now a resident scholar at the Washington-based American Enterprise Institute, says that even today a tobacco company cannot advertise one brand as safer, and these restrictions have made it harder for companies to develop innovations such as low-tar cigarettes that are less harmful.

INEFFECTIVE GOVERNMENT RESTRICTIONS

Whelan thinks advertising does persuade people to start smoking, but doesn't believe government restrictions will be effective. She notes that when France banned cigarette ads, Marlboro circumvented the law by promoting its main product through a line of Marlboro clothing. Whelan, who has frequently joined with conservatives to oppose excessive regulation on environmental issues, says she doesn't believe any federal regulations will be effective in stopping smoking. She parts company with conservatives, however, in saying that the tobacco companies should be held fully liable for the dangers of their products.

"PSST! Hey, kid, want to buy some old magazine
ads of JOE CAMEL?"

Berry's World. Reprinted by permission of NEA, Inc.

Most conservatives, like most juries in cigarette cases, believe that since many of the dangers of smoking have been public knowledge for 30 years, smokers individually assume the risks and aren't entitled to any compensation from tobacco companies. As Jacob Sullum, a nonsmoking libertarian journalist, puts it: "People know that there are risks associated with firearms, alcohol, and swimming pools. They don't know all the details.

Nevertheless, because we've told them this is a dangerous product and you have to be careful with it, we say that they've assumed the risks. It's the same way with cigarettes. I don't think you have to be an expert on the health hazards of smoking in order to have assumed the risks involved with smoking."

Whelan disagrees. She notes that the label on cigarettes is much shorter than those on other products such as over-the-counter drugs and says that a warning label of all the dangers "would have to be as big as a New York City phone book." She says that she would not even consider a skull and crossbones as an acceptable warning and notes that there is a popular novelty brand called Death Cigarettes that uses that very symbol. The only way Whelan would grant cigarette companies immunity from lawsuits is if they get informed consent from smokers.

BANKRUPTING TOBACCO COMPANIES

Some antitobacco activists, however, still won't be satisfied until the companies are bankrupted or get out of the tobacco business. Stanton Glantz, professor of medicine at the University of California-San Francisco, has written that public-health groups shouldn't support a large settlement that does not "bankrupt or otherwise force fundamental changes" in the tobacco industry. Glantz says on a popular antitobacco website that "with patience, enough of the lawsuits facing the industry will succeed to create a situation in which Wall Street will start to pressure Philip Morris, Reynolds and the others to get out of the tobacco business because the liability associated with selling tobacco will jeopardize their nontobacco assets."

In addition to lawsuits, Glantz and other activists also want nearly universal regulation premised on the alleged dangers of tobacco smoke—not just as protection for nonsmokers, but also as harassment to make smokers quit. In an editorial in the *American Journal of Public Health*, Glantz urges health organizations to support the Occupational Safety and Health Administration's proposed rule banning workplace smoking.

Many smokers are already used to putting their packs away at work, on airplanes, or in other public places. But soon they may not be safe even lighting up at home. "The mere fact that they're in their own home or apartment doesn't necessarily mean there's a right to smoke," says George Washington University law professor John Banzhaf, noting that many apartment and condo complexes have cracked down on residential smoking as a result of complaints and lawsuits from residents claiming to be exposed to passive smoke through the ventilation system.

CONTROLLING SMOKING IN THE HOME

Banzhaf, who is also the founder and executive director of Action on Smoking and Health, self-described as the oldest national antismoking organization, speaks with pride about another crackdown on residential smoking he helped to engineer. Banzhaf has called exposing a child to passive smoke the most common form of child abuse and through amicus briefs and legal advice has persuaded 15 courts in 15 states to consider a parent's smoking habit as a factor in custody cases. He says some courts now order parents not to smoke in their homes for up to 48 hours before the child visits.

"In the few cases where the parent has refused to agree not to quit smoking around the child, or where they have violated the order, then courts have stepped in and have taken custody away temporarily or permanently," Banzhaf says.

"We're now moving to the second step," Banzhaf continues. "If we are going to provide protection from second-hand tobacco smoke to children in a divorcing situation, why not protect them also in an intact marriage situation? We now have a small number of situations where outsiders have filed complaints in the nature of child abuse" against parents who smoke around their children. He mentions a Minnesota case in which smoking parents permanently lost custody of their child.

Antismoking-movement critic Sullum predicts that, in the future, about the only people the government may permit to smoke are bachelors in detached houses. When that happens, given the logic of current government policy, the tobacco price-support program will probably still be going strong. And the money grubbing.

PERIODICAL BIBLIOGRAPHY

The following articles have been selected to supplement the diverse views presented in this chapter. Addresses are provided for periodicals not indexed in the *Readers' Guide to Periodical Literature*, the *Alternative Press Index*, the *Social Sciences Index*, or the *Index to Legal Periodicals and Books*.

Dudley Barlow	"How Things Become Invisible," *Education Digest*, January 1998.
Elizabeth Newlin Carney	"Tuning Out Free TV," *National Journal*, April 12, 1997. Available from 1501 M St. NW, Suite 300, Washington, DC 20005.
John Donovan	"They Don't Want What We Have to Sell," *Campaigns & Elections*, April 1997. Available from 1511 K St. NW, Suite 1020, Washington, DC 20005.
Max Frankel	"Pollution Alert," *New York Times Magazine*, May 25, 1997.
Leonard H. Glantz	"Controlling Tobacco Advertising: The FDA Regulations and the First Amendment," *American Journal of Public Health*, March 1997.
Lawrence O. Gostin, Peter S. Arno, and Allan M. Brandt	"FDA Regulation of Tobacco Advertising and Youth Smoking," *JAMA*, February 5, 1997. Available from 515 N. State St., Chicago, IL 60610.
Richard Harwood	"The Alienated American Voter: Are the News Media to Blame?" *Brookings Review*, Fall 1996.
Elizabeth C. Hirschman and Craig J. Thompson	"Why Media Matter: Toward a Richer Understanding on Consumers' Relationships with Advertising and Mass Media," *Journal of Advertising*, Spring 1997. Available from American Academy of Advertising, Clemson University, College of Commerce and Industry, 245 Sirrine Hall, Clemson, SC 29634-1325.
Montague Kern	"Social Capital and Citizen Interpretation of Political Ads, News, and Web Site Information in the 1996 Presidential Elections," *American Behavioral Scientist*, August 1997.
Mary Kuntz	"Is Nothing Sacred?" *Business Week*, May 18, 1998.

| Aaron Mathes | "Culture Jammers," *Dollars and Sense*, November/December 1997. |

| Lori Melton McKinnon et al. | "Policing Political Ads: An Analysis of Five Leading Newspapers' Responses to 1992 Political Advertisements," *Journalism & Mass Communication Quarterly*, Spring 1996. Available from Association for Education in Journalism and Mass Communication, University of South Carolina, Le Conte College, Room 121, Columbia, SC 29208-0251. |

| Irene Costera Meijer | "Advertising Citizenship: An Essay on the Performative Power of Consumer Culture," *Media, Culture & Society*, April 1998. |

| Patrick B. O'Sullivan and Seth Geiger | "Does the Watchdog Bite? Newspaper Ad Watch Articles and Political Attack Ads," *Journalism & Mass Communication Quarterly*, Winter 1995. |

| Jonathan Rowe | "How to Clean Up Campaign Finance, Part 2: Disclose Donors in Political Ads," *U.S. News & World Report*, December 29, 1997. |

| John Tierney | "Why Negative Ads Are Good for Democracy," *New York Times Magazine*, November 3, 1996. |

| Allan Wolper | "Tobacco Targets College Students," *Editor and Publisher*, April 11, 1998. Available from 11 W. 19th St., New York, NY 10011. |

CHAPTER 3

HOW DO THE MEDIA
INFLUENCE POLITICS?

CHAPTER PREFACE

For three centuries, much of American political deliberation occurred in small meeting rooms and town halls. Policy issues were debated face to face. Newspapers, flyers, and magazines were the only "mass media." However, the development of television and radio in the early twentieth century, and the advent of the Internet later in the century, has increasingly swamped the public with news. As a result, the future of democracy may be influenced by the way the media choose to inform the American public and by the way public officials use the media. In his book *Who Deliberates?* Benjamin I. Page writes that "even if the public is capable of a high level of rationality and good sense, public opinion is bound to depend, in good part, upon the political information and ideas that are conveyed to it."

Many political commentators believe that the information provided to the public is inaccurate. Some claim that the news media have a liberal bias that undermines the public's ability to make informed judgments. To support this assertion, they point both to subtle forms of manipulation, like the labeling of conservatives as "extremists," and more overt distortions of political issues. In 1995, the Center for Media and Public Affairs, an organization that studies the news and entertainment media, examined the political coverage of the major television networks and newspapers. The center found that denigrating terms were far more common in the depiction of conservative candidates and elected officials than of liberal politicians.

Others reject the claim that the press has a liberal bias. In 1998, for example, Fairness and Accuracy in Reporting (FAIR) released a poll of journalists showing that in reporting on economic issues, the media are actually more conservative than the general public. Columnist Jeff Cohen contends that media fail to cover stories of interest to liberals. If the media had a liberal bias, he insists, the public would be bombarded with articles about the "tax shift from wealthy individuals and corporations to middle-class and working-class people." The fact that these stories do not reach the public, he argues, is evidence that the liberal bias of the press is a myth.

Media bias is among the issues debated in the following chapter on media coverage of political issues.

| "Political liberals are much more heavily represented among people working for the major media than among the general public."

THE MEDIA HAVE A LIBERAL BIAS

Allan Levite

In the following viewpoint, Allan Levite argues that political liberals are treated much more sympathetically by the major news media than are political conservatives. He draws this conclusion from a number of quantitative studies showing that words critical of conservatives appear much more frequently in news reports than words critical of liberals. The author believes that this liberal bias stems in part from the fact that liberals are drawn to the profession of journalism. Levite is a research fellow at the Independent Institute in Oakland, California, and the author of *Guilt and Politics*.

As you read, consider the following questions:
1. According to the author, what did a search of the Lexis/Nexis database reveal about biased terms in journalistic sources?
2. What evidence does Levite provide that people who feel guilty about their work are more likely to be liberal?
3. How do today's journalists compare to those of the past, in the author's opinion?

I s there a prevailing liberal bias among the major news media? Until now, this has been largely a matter of opinion. Conservatives typically complain of it, while liberals often deny its existence. It is usually admitted, however, that political liberals are much more heavily represented among people working for the major media than among the general public. The well-known study by S. Robert Lichter, Stanley Rothman, and Linda Richter, *The Media Elite*, based on in-depth interviews with 238 major-media journalists, found that liberals outnumbered conservatives by 54 per cent to 17 per cent. A nationwide *Los Angeles Times* study (August 11, 1985) administered its own poll to 3,000 reporters and editors and got almost exactly the same result: 55 per cent liberal and 17 per cent conservative. (The *Times* survey, which also polled 3,000 members of the general public, found that in the latter group 24 per cent were liberal, 29 per cent conservative, and 33 per cent "neither," a striking contrast to the findings for journalists.)

CD-ROM Searches

Although this liberal tilt is usually acknowledged by the major media, it is often said that professional standards prevent it from translating into news bias. Many efforts have been made to put this claim to the test. But analyzing network news for bias is very difficult, since any in-depth research would require the tape recording of all three major networks simultaneously, and the assessment of news content would involve some interpretation. However, thanks to the invention of the CD-ROM and computer databases, it is now possible to test the print media for ideological bias by simply performing word-count searches for favorable and unfavorable labels.

For example, the word "activist" implies dedication, effort, and sincerity. The word "extremist" implies fanaticism, intolerance, and possibly even violence. If liberal media bias is prevalent, a search of media sources would find the word "activist" applied to liberals far more often than to conservatives, while the word "extremist" would be applied to conservatives much more often than to liberals.

Searches of the ProQuest full-text CD-ROM listings reveal that between January 1994 and March 1995, the *New York Times* had 289 articles that applied the word "activist" to liberals, liberal causes, or the Left. Only 65 applied it to conservatives or conservative causes. This is a ratio of 4.4 to 1. The term "extremist" was used by the same source in only 25 articles referring to liberalism, but in 78 articles referring to conservatism, a 3 to 1 ratio.

A search of the Lexis/Nexis newspaper database of about 170 publications shows the phrases "conservative attack" and "conservative criticism" occurring 4.2 times more often than "liberal attack" and "liberal criticism." Similarly, "Republican attack" and "Republican criticism" occurred 2.9 times more often than "Democratic attack" and "Democratic criticism."

The prefix "arch," applied to people, is generally unfavorable. "Arch-traitor" and "arch-villain" are fairly common expressions, but not "arch-patriot" or "arch-hero." Such terms as "arch-enemy" or "arch-nemesis" are commonly used, but not "arch-friend" or "arch-ally." The print media used the terms "archconservative" and "arch conservative" more than "archliberal" and "arch liberal" (both variations were included in the count) by a ratio of 20 to 1.

Furthermore, the key phrases far right, extreme right, and radical right are found almost twice as often as far left, extreme left, and radical left. Because Lexis/Nexis goes back as far as 1977 (in the case of the *Washington Post*), 1980 (for the *New York Times* and the *Christian Science Monitor*), and 1985 (for the *Chicago Tribune* and the *Los Angeles Times*), whatever right-wing extremism developed during the early-to-mid 1990s could not have been a major cause of this slant. Indeed, the same database shows the phrase "right wing" occurring more than 153,000 times, far more often than "left wing." These milder phrases do not necessarily refer to bomb-throwing extremists; they often refer to politicians, writers, and academics. Much the same can be said for the key word "ultra-conservative" and its variant, "ultra conservative," which occurs 3.7 times more often than "ultraliberal" and "ultra liberal."

Adding the results of the searches for the key words far right/extreme right/radical right and far left/extreme left/radical left, the ProQuest General Periodicals index showed a 4 to 1 ratio for 1993–94 (122 to 30); a 2.77 to 1 ratio for the 1990–92 (236 to 85); and a 2.4 to 1 ratio for 1986–89 (272 to 113). While these ratios have been increasing, they were already above 2 to 1 in the mid-to-late 1980s. In addition, there is the Public Affairs Information Service (PAIS) International Database, which includes books, journal articles, government documents, and committee reports all the way back to 1972. A PAIS search performed in the fall of 1995 showed a ratio of 2.28 to 1 between far right/extreme right/radical right and far left/extreme left/radical left. . . .

GUILT OF INACTION

The question of why media bias is so pervasive must focus on why the political views of journalists—particularly major-media journalists—are so different from those of the public at large. Obviously, the journalists' occupation and social position play a key role, since their political views resemble the views of writers and academics, not the views of blue-collar workers.

A LIBERAL REPORTING BIAS

Every public policy, whether liberal or conservative, has some proponents motivated by principle and others by selfishness. Liberal policies, such as promoting government regulation of political speech, are consistently reported as principled and unselfish. Conservative policies, such as opposing government regulation of political speech, are consistently reported as unprincipled and selfish.

Media Research Center, *Medianomics*, July 1998.

Managerial psychologist Harry Levinson has suggested that "With less physiological work, less handling of materials, and less action for some people, the function of work as an atonement device may be lost. People who are not working feel guilty. If work seemingly makes fewer demands on them, that makes them uneasy." Artists, writers, actors, and academics may be susceptible to guilt about not having to perform arduous manual labor even if they are not actually wealthy. And among those who are rich, the situation is often aggravated. Peggy Rockefeller and Laura Rockefeller were members of the far-left Students for a Democratic Society. Peggy's cousin Marion Weber actually hoped that a revolution would come along and relieve her of her wealth. Alida Rockefeller was also attracted to radicalism, and Abby Rockefeller was smitten with Marxism. Josephine Drexel Biddle Duke, who led a violent demonstration against Secretary of State Dean Rusk, was descended from James Duke, founder of the giant American Tobacco Company. For persons who regret occupying this socio-economic stratum, egalitarian politics offers a way out: if the embarrassing contrast between social positions is reduced or eliminated, there would be much less reason to feel uncomfortable about not being poor, or not being a manual laborer.

How closely do metropolitan and major-media journalists fit this profile? Three factors are involved. First of all, they often receive large salaries. A 1985 *Los Angeles Times* poll showed that only 18 per cent of the general public earned over $40,000, but over half of the newspaper journalists did. According to *The Media Elite*, by 1990 the starting salary for *New York Times* reporters exceeded

$50,000; the average *Washington Post* reporter received nearly $60,000. At the three major networks, news anchors may now earn over $1 million per year; even some local anchors now do.

A CUSHY JOB

Second, journalism itself is a cushy and enjoyable job that always has many more applicants than openings.

Third, major-media journalists report what is happening in the world but do not participate in it. As the Associated Press's former General Manager Wes Gallagher has observed, a reporter records events but is divorced from them.

All of this supports the conclusion that most journalists, especially those in the major media, will be liberals. Political doctrines that promise to alleviate social inequities would have special value for them, because any lessening of the gulf between the comfortable and the deprived would reduce the philosophical uneasiness of the comfortable. This situation did not always hold true among journalists, but the further they have moved away from the workaday world, the more pronounced it has become.

It is sometimes claimed that journalists become liberals by being continually exposed to news about crime, poverty, and other social problems, the understandable response to which is a bias toward reformist viewpoints. If this were true, however, older journalists would be more liberal than their younger colleagues, having been exposed to such unsettling reports for a longer period. But the Lichter-Rothman surveys mentioned earlier showed that younger journalists are considerably more liberal than their older counterparts. Anyway, if the "exposure" reasoning were correct, we could expect all the reports about government misdeeds and scandals to have turned the majority of journalists into libertarians or anarchists by now.

WHISKY-DRINKING JOURNALISM

In the past, there were many conservative commentators and newspapers. But those were also the days of hard-bitten, whisky-drinking, seat-of-the-pants journalism, hardly resembling the present-day variety. Media luminary Ben Bagdikian, in fact, has written that before World War II journalism was a way for working-class people to advance themselves, and that college educations were seldom required and may even have been a disadvantage. In 1936, only 51 per cent of reporters in Washington, D.C., were college graduates. Today, 93 per cent have degrees. The profession today is characterized by journalists and editors whose values differ markedly from the values both of their scrappy predecessors and of the masses.

Because of the unique socio-economic situation of journalists, the professional standards of the nation's newspapers have been unable to prevent the wholesale slanting of the news in the directions indicated above. It remains to be seen whether the media will act to restore the political balance that they acknowledge is needed. The first step would be to abandon their efforts to deny that this bias exists.

"Rush Limbaugh alone gets more electronic exposure than all the lefties on the continent."

THE MEDIA DO NOT HAVE A LIBERAL BIAS

Richard Reeves

In the following viewpoint, Richard Reeves responds to the common charge that the news media have a liberal bias. He contends that while journalists tend to be culturally liberal, most are relatively conservative politically and have a professional interest in maintaining objectivity. Moreover, he maintains, the views of conservatives receive extensive coverage in the mainstream media. Reeves, a former regents professor of political science at UCLA, is a syndicated columnist and former chief political correspondent for the *New York Times*. His many books include *Do the Media Govern: Politicians, Voters, and Reporters in America*, coedited with Shanto Iyengar.

As you read, consider the following questions:

1. According to the author, what common characteristics are shared by the "royalty of journalism"?
2. According to Reeves, how did William E. Simon help get conservative ideas into the mainstream?
3. What does the author mean when he writes that the conservative intelligentsia "are political activists, not political chroniclers"?

A great deal is made of the so-called "liberal press," but the liberalism of the elite press is more cultural than political. The royalty of journalism pretty much shares the social attitudes of other well-educated and high-earning Americans, beginning with an aversion to progressive income taxes.

Cokie Roberts of ABC News, it is true, is the daughter of two Democratic members of Congress, Hale Boggs, the late majority leader of the House, and his widow, former Representative Lindy Boggs. Tim Russert, the Washington bureau chief of NBC News and moderator of *Meet the Press*, served on the staffs of two prominent New York Democrats, Senator Daniel Patrick Moynihan and Governor Mario Cuomo. But William Safire of *The New York Times*, John McLaughlin, the television ringmaster, Diane Sawyer of ABC, and David Gergen of *U.S. News & World Report*, all served together on President Richard Nixon's staff—and, at the time, Nixon was trying to hire Robert Bartley, a young editorial writer on *The Wall Street Journal* who became a Pulitzer-Prize winning voice of the right. Sam Donaldson of ABC, energetic defender of the little guy, gets more than $100,000 a year in federal agricultural subsidies for a sheep ranch he owns in New Mexico.

Are they biased? Of course—who isn't?

A CLOAK AND A GOAL

That bias of the ladies and gentlemen of the press, however, is less than politicians and millions of Americans seem to think. Journalists, like politicians, are anxious to preserve their own popularity and credibility. Both reporters and pundits generally have to deal with both sides of an issue or all sides of ongoing political struggles and they are usually even more anxious to keep the respect of their peers. "Objectivity" is both a cloak and a goal for journalists—most cannot make a living if they are not seen by sources, readers, viewers, and bosses as trying to be fair.

That is at least the way it has been for most of the people most of the time. In the late 1960s, young liberals stormed the business, arguing that there was no "other side" on issues like war and poverty and race relations. Most of them soon faded into moderation or obscurity. Then, in the 1980s a wave of conservative thinkers, writers, and "journalists" emerged, many of them complaining that they were being ignored or suppressed by liberal elites.

They were right, in a sense. They were being shunned, not politically but culturally.

All celebrity is created equal in the electronic zoo, so it has become perfectly natural to see things like former Vice President

Dan Quayle substituting for Larry King on CNN. The journalists being interviewed were quick to say that "the media" takes great pains to be fair. "I'm not saying that it's not fair," said Quayle, "but it's fair through the liberal prism."

Most liberals, me among them, agree we may have a prism but they, the conservatives, seem to have bigger megaphones. Rush Limbaugh alone gets more electronic exposure than all the lefties on the continent. Anybody with a dollar can find out what Safire or George Will, a former Republican congressional staffer, or the editorial writers of The Wall Street Journal think most every day of the year. The nonfiction best-seller list of the 1990s was generally dominated by provocative conservative authors. Even public television was projecting more and more faces of the right; people like William F. Buckley and Peggy Noonan replaced the liberals who found a home there years ago. A "Christian conservative," Pat Robertson, has his own channel.

GETTING IDEAS INTO THE MAINSTREAM

Conservatives, in obvious fact, have done a tremendous job in getting their ideas across in the mainstream media. Much of the credit for that should go to William E. Simon, the Wall Streeter who was secretary of the treasury to two Republican presidents. His 1978 book, a best-seller titled A Time for Truth, ended with a strategy that worked: "I know of nothing more crucial than to come to the aid of the intellectuals and writers who are fighting on my side. . . . A powerful counterintelligentsia can be organized to challenge our ruling [liberal] opinion makers . . . an audience awaits its [conservative] views."

So it did. Simon urged corporate America to use its "public affairs" contributions to support intellectuals of the right—in journalism, universities and think tanks. To show the way, he used a foundation he controlled, the John M. Olin Foundation, to create university chairs and such for conservative thinkers, such as Irving Kristol and Allan Bloom, and to encourage the creation and financing of independent right-wing college newspapers to recruit and train a new generation of bright conservative writers.

A CULTURAL BIAS

It worked brilliantly. The new conservative generation, however—the winners in ideological wars—whined that liberals still run the world of ideas. Quayle got the beginning of the answer on the King show from Tim Russert. "I think there's more of a cultural bias than a political bias," said NBC News's main man in

Washington. That is it exactly. Like Rodney Dangerfield, conservative thinkers don't get no respect. They may be admired for their political impact or envied for their corporate and foundation support, but they are not respected or affirmed intellectually by a cultural elite more "liberal" than most middle-class voters.

Sidewalk Bubblegum ©98 Clay Butler. Reprinted with permission.

In addition, no matter how smart or literate or successful they are, the new conservative intelligentsia—or counterintelligentsia—do not deserve cultural affirmation. They are political activists, not political chroniclers or commentators. You can learn from them, but you cannot trust them. At their best, which can be very good indeed, *Wall Street Journal* editorials, the *American Spectator* "exposes," the books of Charles Murray, and the asides of P.J. O'Rourke compile only information that "works" for their side. They are pamphleteers, not essayists.

In the 1990s, they have not been able to have it both ways. The cultural bias that bothers conservative thinkers (and Quayle) is real—it is the perverse bent of thinkers and writers who inevitably sell out their friends when they are wrong or foolish.

The scorned "liberals" could seem pathetic when they beat up on Bill Clinton or any other ideological companion who actually has power. That is the point, however: Cultural respect and affirmation come from choosing argument over power—and so far the new conservative intelligentsia seems incapable of biting the hands that feed them so well.

| "We must ask ourselves whether
incessant election polling furthers
the goals and ideals of democracy, or
merely the financial and competitive
interests of media companies."

OPINION POLLS ARE BAD FOR POLITICS

Part I: Robert Kubey and Vincent M. Fitzgerald,
Part II: Godfrey Sperling

In Part I of the following two-part viewpoint, Robert Kubey and Vincent M. Fitzgerald argue that public opinion polls harm political campaigns by focusing media attention on the popularity of candidates rather than on important political issues, and by unfairly aiding front-runners. In Part II, Godfrey Sperling contends that polls have become part of the democratic process and can potentially distort the outcome of elections. Kubey is the director of the masters program in communication and information studies at Rutgers University in New Brunswick, New Jersey. Fitzgerald is an assistant professor of communications at the College of Mount Saint Vincent in Riverdale, New York. Sperling is an editorial writer for the *Christian Science Monitor*.

As you read, consider the following questions:

1. Why has the press become so interested in reporting the results of polls, according to Kubey and Fitzgerald?
2. What attitudes did Sperling learn from his father concerning polls?

Part I: Reprinted from Robert Kubey and Vincent M. Fitzgerald, "Poll-Happy Media Need to Cool It," *The Christian Science Monitor*, October 29, 1996, by permission of the authors. Part II: Reprinted from Godfrey Sperling, "If They Took a Poll About Polls," *The Christian Science Monitor*, November 12, 1996, with permission from *The Christian Science Monitor*.

I

Polling during presidential election campaigns has become a daily affair with unfortunate consequences for voters and politicians alike. Not only has the number of voter polls broadcast by network television news more than tripled since 1968, our research shows that polling reports have grown at the expense of issue coverage.

In 1968, for each minute of poll coverage in their news reports, the TV networks broadcast four minutes of campaign issue coverage. By 1992 this ratio had fallen to only 90 seconds of issue coverage for each minute of poll coverage.

NEWS EXCLUSIVES

These changes are not an accident. Television news producers believe that to hold viewer interest they must de-emphasize issue coverage and turn campaigns into horse races. Indeed, we've found that poll results in the 1990s are much more likely to be reported at the beginning of broadcasts as "news exclusives" than they were in the 1960s and '70s. This helps create the impression that the network has landed a scoop and that the story being reported is especially important and newsworthy.

Network news executives typically blame the public, rather than themselves, for this lack of issue orientation in their broadcasts. "People hate politics," they complain. "Viewers will change channels if we report on issues." But polling and constant horse-race coverage contribute to the public's lack of involvement and experience with campaign issues. Polls are used to characterize how each candidate and campaign is doing, but with little awareness that they often drive the whole tone and orientation of stories.

SOUND-BITE SATURATION

Of course, poll-generated stories also have enormous impact on the candidates' campaigns. Positive polls fuel enthusiasm and confidence for a front-runner, while negative poll reports cause campaign contributions to decline, endorsements to fall off, and staff energy and morale to wither.

Constant poll reporting also makes it much more difficult for the underdog to get his message out. Instead of being allowed to focus on issues and positions, the trailing candidate is hounded by reporters asking him to explain his poor showing in the polls and whether he will change his strategy.

Walter Mondale in 1984, Michael Dukakis in 1988, and

George Bush in 1992 each faced one disparaging poll-driven question after another, as did Bob Dole in 1996. The questioning and the stories become self-perpetuating. Negative stories and sound bites saturate the news, contributing to the decided view of the underdog as ineffectual, a certain loser, even though these stories would never have been broadcast or written had the same candidate been leading in the polls.

Polls can also reduce the appetite of reporters to do tough stories on the front-runner. Because correspondents are often convinced of the outcome weeks before election day, some will back away from highly critical stories about the front-runner in the final days of a campaign knowing that they need to maintain good working relations with the new or reelected administration. Conversely, there is little or no such restraint shown toward the underdog because it is assumed that he and his staff will soon be virtually irrelevant as news sources.

ROBBING THE VOTERS

Pre-election poll projections also rob voters of the sense that they are part of the process. In those instances where the presidential election may be the only significant contest on a ballot, one can understand why some citizens may choose not to vote if the news media have spent weeks chanting the same mantra that the outcome is already certain.

Just as the television networks claim that their election-day predictions based in exit-polling are completely benign—even though millions of voters in the Far West are routinely told by the networks that the presidential election has already been decided before the polls in their states have even closed—news organizations remain oblivious to their role in shaping the tenor of our electoral politics through incessant preelection polling.

Recognizing these problems, other countries have outlawed polling altogether, or for the final few weeks of an election. Such a solution seems extreme to some, and in the United States it would fly in the face of the First Amendment. Ideally, news organizations would stop conducting so many polls, and editors and reporters would exercise much greater restraint in using polls to both shape coverage and spike audience ratings and reader interest.

Although the competitive and dramatic elements of a campaign may often be more exciting, they are less substantive. We must ask ourselves whether incessant election polling furthers the goals and ideals of democracy, or merely the financial and competitive interests of media companies.

II

Is it any wonder that there wasn't much enthusiasm being shown over a [1996 presidential] race where we had known for months who would win? Very early on, the pollsters were telling us that President Clinton would win handily over Bob Dole—and they kept telling us that right up to election time. The hard campaigning had changed nothing. "Clinton in a walk," we were told.

So with no great zest we went out and voted, already knowing the result. And then we turned on the TV, at least for a while, to watch the anticipated Clinton victory become validated by the actual count. If we stayed up, it was to see how the Senate and House contests or other local races or issues were being decided.

TAKING THE FUN OUT OF ELECTIONS

But the pollsters, as they so often do, had taken all the suspense—all the fun—out of the presidential election.

When I was a youngster back in the '20s, I got the distinct impression, mostly from my father, that polls weren't permissible in the way we elected people in our country. He told me that polls interfered with our democratic processes. He said they were evil, and I think he even told me they were illegal. Dad may have overstated the bad status of polls, but I have never gotten over the feeling that he was right.

MISINTERPRETING THE POLLS

The news media often misrepresent or misinterpret polls either because they take them too literally or because, at the other extreme, they underestimate their technical complexity. It is important to remember (1) that projections from election surveys are uncertain because many people change their minds and some who say they will vote do not; (2) that all surveys are subject to errors that go beyond the laws of chance; and (3) that survey statistics arise from a series of professional judgments; just because they come out of a computer does not make them right.

Leo Bogart, *Society*, May/June 1998.

Pollsters claim they are useful, that they very accurately portray voter attitudes and intentions. They go on to trumpet that politicians and political writers couldn't get along without them and that the public is greatly benefited by the information they mine and bring to the surface.

I know that as a newsman I have leaned heavily on poll results as a reference point for telling readers what candidate appears to be winning and who is behind. Over the years the polls have become very reliable. But when I was covering presidential campaigns, I always preferred to do my own checking on voter attitudes. That was when I was going all around the country, talking to a lot of people in different walks of life. More recently, I have ceased this grass-roots reporting. So, regretfully, I do rely heavily—and doubtless too much—on the findings of polls.

DISTORTING THE VOTING PROCESS

But my suspicion is that Dad was right—that polls are anathema to the voting process. I can't prove it, but I think these polls take on a life of themselves. For example, a poll that shows Mr. Clinton is ahead of Mr. Dole (as polls actually were showing when the campaign began) will have some kind of an effect on the race. It could dampen the spirits of those in the Dole camp and encourage the Clintonites. Or it could spur the efforts of the Dole people and make for complacency in the Clinton camp.

If these polls persist, showing Clinton's big lead still present at election time (as was the case), it could well cause many Dole supporters to stay home, saying "what's the use?" Or it could cause Clinton's fans to decide that their votes weren't needed.

I'm not sure of what poll results do. But they do something that distorts our process. They become a part of the election. And, again, I can't prove it, but I think that these insertions of poll results and findings can even turn elections completely around. We'll never know.

Polls are likely here to stay, much to my regret, particularly since they are taking all the fun out of these presidential elections by telling us who will win before we vote.

Sometimes all we have to hope for is that the pollsters will, somehow, be embarrassed by the outcome. Actually, the popular vote result between Clinton and Dole was closer than the pollsters had predicted—but not enough to cause any of them to express any shame over their performance.

| *"As researchers, [political pollsters]*
| *make an important contribution to*
| *a democratic society."*

OPINION POLLS ARE GOOD FOR POLITICS

Andrew Kohut

In the following viewpoint, Andrew Kohut responds to criticisms commonly made about the use of opinion polls in politics and the news coverage of political races. He notes that the public, the press, and policy makers are all skeptical of opinion polls for different reasons. The author contends that these criticisms are mostly unfounded and that, in fact, opinion polls provide information that can help politicians become responsible leaders. Kohut calls on pollsters to be more eloquent in defense of polling. Kohut is director of the Times Mirror Center for the People and the Press. The following viewpoint was excerpted from a speech delivered to the American Association for Public Opinion Research.

As you read, consider the following questions:

1. What reasons does Kohut give for the public's skepticism toward polls?
2. How does the public view polls and pollsters, according to the author?
3. According to the viewpoint, why was Lindsay Rogers's criticism of polls so important?
4. What, according to Kohut, did Edwin Bernays mean when he said that opinion polls were like icebergs? How did Harry Field respond to this criticism?

Excerpted from Andrew Kohut, "Opinion Polls and the Democratic Process," *Public Opinion Quarterly*, vol. 59, no. 3 (Fall 1995), p. 463. Copyright © American Association for Public Opinion Research, 1995. Reprinted by permission of the author and the University of Chicago Press.

I have spent my entire professional life designing, conducting, and reporting attitude surveys. I had the pleasure of working with two of the three acknowledged founding fathers of public opinion polling, George Gallup and Archibald Crossley. But more important, I had the good fortune of being trained by the much less acknowledged Paul Perry. Perry, who devised the Gallup Organization's election methodology, was chiefly responsible for its remarkable polling record between 1950 and 1980. A record that helped restore credibility to all opinion polls, post-1948.

I think it is fair to say that I can trace my research roots in opinion research back to the early days of opinion polling, and the early days of the American Association for Public Opinion Research (AAPOR).

DEMOCRACY AND PUBLIC OPINION

I like what I do, and I believe that as researchers, we make an important contribution to a democratic society. But increasingly, many outside our profession either have begun to doubt this or flatly disagree that America is a better place because of opinion research. The new criticisms of polls differ from the criticisms that I heard when I first started coming to AAPOR. They are not about our methods, or our accuracy as they once were, but are now about our impact upon the democratic process.

The founders of the survey research profession felt strongly that American democracy benefited from what they did, and they articulated it just as simply as that. We don't. We are not nearly as much advocates of polling as was the first generation of survey researchers. And that is troubling because our critics are growing in number and our professional image has been transformed.

I don't think we have the Rodney Dangerfield problem. Polls get plenty of respect. But they get very little affection. Polls get respect because their results are a source of power, particularly in Washington, where I work. But they are not well liked for a variety of reasons, depending on the perspective of the critic. All of us have our own examples and anecdotes about the way pollsters are portrayed in the popular culture—either as manipulators themselves or as advisers to weak officials. And, during an election period, talk to civic groups, or just plain folks, about polling and feel the vibes. They are not very good. When I first started giving such talks people would ask how we do it; now they ask why we do it.

As I see it, the people, the press, and the policymakers all voice different, but in many ways interrelated, concerns about the polls.

THE PEOPLE

The public thinks that polls are used by politicians and campaigners to manipulate the electorate. Added to what I call frustrations with forecasting, the public now also faults polling as an integral part of the new politics of sound bites, negative campaigning, media blitzes, and so on. Writing in 1995 in the *New York Times*, Michael Wines described the public as regarding pollsters as "puppet-masters, dictating policy by telling Presidents and Congressmen what will and what won't win votes." He added that pollsters are "the sorcerers of modern politics" and quoted Bill Schneider describing pollsters as having the "reputation of Svengalis," because in his words the "pollster is supposed to have some mystic communion with the American electorate."

Clearly, the antagonism toward pollsters is part and parcel of a larger discontent with politics and governance. The prominence of partisan polling in campaigning these days plays no small part in this. Many of the most negative aspects of our public image emanate from the role that partisan pollsters play. While they employ the survey method and rely on data to come to their conclusions, their highest priorities are getting their clients elected and keeping them in office. The acuity of their recommendations is more important than the accuracy of their data. Many do solid survey work. In my opinion, many more do mediocre to poor survey work, but their skill as consultants compensates for these shortcomings. They have been doing it the wrong way for so long, many of them don't know what they don't know.

The media practice of bipartisan pairing of pollsters only detracts from the public image of pollsters. Even when they are discussing well-conducted surveys, two are required to offset the biases of one. Listening to them spin and spar, rather than illuminate, can only leave the public with more doubts about the survey enterprise.

THE PRESS AND POLICYMAKERS

I don't mean to single out partisan polling as the cause of all of our problems. Many in the press and elsewhere are critical of the way published polls have changed campaign coverage. Horse-race journalism is what every serious news organization does not want to practice. The impact of fund-raising on a candidate's standing in published polls and polls as news making, rather than as news reporting, are the frequent complaints about the published polls. Alfred Cantril does a good job of covering such criticisms in his book *The Opinion Connection.*

In recent years concerns about the impact of public opinion polling on governance have increased markedly. Criticisms of the Clinton administration for its reliance on opinion polling and a campaign approach within the White House are in part responsible. There is no shortage of columns and editorials that make the point that true leaders are not poll driven. A large element of this has to do with the highly visible role that Stan Greenberg and now new pollsters play in the affairs of the Clinton administration. In *On the Edge,* Elizabeth Drew writes, "Previous Presidents had pollsters and other outside political advisers, but never before had they played such an integral part in a Presidency. . . . The amount of weight given in presidential decision making to polling results can have a defining effect on a Presidency."

PUBLIC OPINION IS COHERENT AND STABLE

One of the core ideas of democracy is that governments ought to do what their citizens want them to do. Or, to put it another way, governments ought to pay attention to public opinion, ought to respond to the policy preferences of the people. I am a strong believer in democracy. In *The Rational Public,* Robert Shapiro and I argued that—despite the fears of some of the Founding Fathers like Alexander Hamilton, and contrary to warnings from pundits and scholars like Walter Lippmann— Americans' collective policy preferences are actually well worth paying attention to. Public opinion is generally coherent and consistent. It flows from Americans' basic values, and it is mostly sensible—sometimes more sensible than the views of those who set themselves up as leaders or experts. Public opinion is usually stable, as well, except that it reacts in reasonable ways to world events and to new information that is presented to it.

Benjamin I. Page, *Who Deliberates? Mass Media in Modern Democracy,* 1996.

Indeed, but the reverse is true as well. The way a president uses polls can affect, and in this case is affecting, the way polls are thought of. Having looked at recent critiques and other major quarrels with polling over the past decade, I catalog their themes as follows.

1. Public opinion polls subvert leadership—the familiar refrain that surveys convert leaders into followers. A good recent example is Robin Gerber writing in the *Washington Post* that "polls corrupt the leader's instinct to govern from the guts." She

quotes Congressman Steny Hoyer saying, "Surveys confuse leaders. . . . We are not trying to figure out what's right but what is the passion of the day." In the area of foreign policy, analysts cite the marriage of polling and real-time television reporting as a one-two punch that holds leaders hostage to instant referendums on decisions about international events that people watch on CNN.

The Case Against Polls

2. Polls create a climate of opinion and are used to manipulate the public. In a *Harper's* piece that attracted a lot of attention, Christopher Hitchens describes polling as "a malignancy that its early critics could not have imagined." He sees surveys as "borne out of a struggle not to discover public opinion, but to master it." From his left-wing perspective he writes that "the polling industry is a powerful ally of depoliticalization, and its counterpart, which is consensus." He adds that, while polls help decide what people think, "their most important long-term influence may be on how people think."

A decade earlier, from the Right, Irving Kristol had written a slightly more measured but similar critique. He saw a conspiracy between the establishment media and polls to create a liberal consensus, complaining that the polls were keeping the Reagan administration from doing the right thing in Central America. Ironically, Hitchens also uses Central America, but as an example of how public opinion polls are sometimes consciously downplayed when their results don't fit a policy objective.

3. Polls promote majoritism. Renewed interest in town hall meetings and direct democracy has given new life to this complaint. For example, in a 1995 monograph about the impact of polling on journalism, Alison Carper writes that "when polls dictate policy, the boundaries of representational government are being breached." Quoting Hume and Locke, she writes that the public is far too predisposed to its own interests to put them ahead of the common good. An argument that she raises against overreliance on what the public thinks in a number of venues—ranging from what kind of newspaper to publish to what kind of laws to enact.

4. Polls measure nonopinions. Why should the views of respondents who know little and have thought less about complicated issues be taken seriously? A good recent example in the *Houston Chronicle* editorial page complained of muddled poll results about the 104th Congress. It explained to its readers that "a major drawback in basing policy on polling data is that many of

those polled have not thought long and deeply on the complicated issues about which they are being asked. And the typical pollster does not encourage reflection before response."

We certainly see a lot of these complaints these days, but I was struck by how similar they are to the critiques of polling 50 years ago. One of the first things that I did in preparation for this talk was to look at what outsiders were saying about the polls as AAPOR came to life. Lindsay Rogers was the most famous poll basher of that era. It was he who named us "pollsters" in his book of that title, which railed against all aspects of polling from the very idea of defining public opinion to specific survey methods. Gallup's *Public Opinion Quarterly* (POQ) response was that "Rogers contradicted himself in every chapter." "But the book served one useful purpose: . . . within its covers one will find a compendium of all the criticisms ever voiced against polls. I would require every student in a public opinion course to read it."

As entertaining as *The Pollsters* and Gallup's responses were, I was more taken by the view of polling offered 50 years ago in *Public Opinion Quarterly* by Edwin Bernays and the responses to this piece in a subsequent POQ by Claude Robinson, Paul Lazarsfeld, and Harry Field. Bernays, an influential public relations figure, saw many good things in polling, but worried that polls were "potentially dangerous weapons in the hands of the unwise, the inept or the dishonest."

A Tool to Aid Democracy

He worried that (1) polls often lull leaders into the belief that they are safe from disapproval when quantitative percentages corroborate their own point of view; (2) polls have produced a leadership that is led by polls and destroys progressive action; they help maintain the status quo; (3) the voice of the people is portrayed as seemingly unchangeable in polls; and (4) public opinion is like an iceberg—the visible portion is the expressed attitudes, but the submerged portion is sometimes more powerful.

Bernays went on to say that the true function of attitude polls is to be a tool to aid leaders to fulfill their democratic function. He made a distinction between crystallized opinions and loosely held ones, which leaders or any other influence can affect.

By today's standards this was a relatively mild and reasoned set of criticisms, but AAPOR's leadership responded sharply, and in the way that clearly reflected who they were. Lazarsfeld was struck by the variance between the undertone of the article and its literal content. He accused Bernays of not liking the polls. Nonetheless, he closed his response by saying that he was applying to Bernays for funds to study how to better educate readers and users of polls (one of Bernays's two ways of dealing with the problems he detailed).

Robinson, a good businessman and a good Republican who founded the Opinion Research Corporation (ORC), one of the leading commercial firms of the 1940s, 1950s, and 1960s, decried the idea of licensing pollsters, Bernays's other recommendation. In Robinson's words, "there is a high premium on honesty in public opinion research," which was self-policed given the interplay between polling organizations and their clientele. "Laissez polling"—so to speak.

Field said Bernays was "on dangerous ground" himself in pointing a finger at polls as potentially dangerous, "because the very same finger could be pointed at religion, freedom of the press and speech, and the democratic process itself." However, he did go on to say that he liked the iceberg metaphor.

MAPPING THE POLITICAL MINEFIELD

The pioneers of polling were quick to come to the defense of their work, particularly when those criticisms dealt with the impact of polls on society. I don't see that same response today from the polling community. We are more apt to defend our techniques, and the reliability of our findings, than we are to take on those who raise the points I have been discussing. In fact, the only recent major defense of the role of public opinion polls has been made by historian Garry Wills in the New York Times Magazine, not too long ago.

Wills, in a very good presentation, points out that complaints about lack of leadership are common in every period of history and that accusing leaders of being followers because they watch polls is an oversimplification. He describes leadership as a balancing act, with polls showing good leaders how to juggle conflicting demands, and how to walk through the minefields. He wrote, "Can a politician know too much about the mood and thinking out there? It seems obscurantist to say so. The great leader uses every kind of knowledge that can be had."

He goes on to say that even if there were no polls there would be some system of handicapping. And he provides a historical context in saying that "the power of public opinion existed long before the arrival of formal polling."

With regard to the president he says "some who say that Clinton listens too much, may not like what the polls are saying." He closes his article by recalling Lyndon B. Johnson. "He learned that politicians live or die by the polls, one way or another—principally by the way they use them. If they refuse to use the polls, they end up with the polls using them."

Why did such an eloquent defense of our role in society and our impact on leadership come from a historian, and not from a survey researcher? Are we not hearing what others are saying? Do we agree more with our critics than Gallup, Roper, and Field did 50 years ago? Are we not as self-confident? . . .

To conclude, I want to refer back to a 1957 special edition of *Public Opinion Quarterly* that was devoted to the first 20 years of public opinion research. Most of the major polling figures, social scientists, and commercial researchers gave their perspectives on the new enterprise of survey research in that volume. But I was most taken by the thoughts of William Albig, a University of Illinois sociologist, because they were so prophetic. He observed that over the first 2 decades of survey research, methods had been refined, but the capacity for insightful generalization had atrophied.

In writing of the rise of the manipulator researcher (as he termed it), he said that "a loss of respect for their target, the common man, was an inevitable occupational hazard. Moreover, during the next 20 years, the common man will inevitably appear to be even more uniformed, intellectually defenseless, and sentimentally maudlin, as he is increasingly belabored by interest groups using modern mass media."

He went on to say, "I do not believe in the romantic idealization or defense of the abilities or potentialities of the common man." But, he added, most of America's political philosophers who were also practicing statesmen quite properly exhibited confidence in the sentiments of the general public. Large publics preserve the sentiments of the culture in which they live, and frequently exhibit the ability to choose with reasonable accuracy among the proposals which come from leaders and from that stratum of the general public which is more broadly knowledgeable.

I believe this too. I think we have to do a better job defending that ability from those who doubt it. And do a better job in our research of reflecting the ability of the public to make wise judgments.

| "Candidates should be able to talk to voters based on the strength of their ideas, not the size of their pocketbooks."

POLITICAL CANDIDATES SHOULD RECEIVE FREE TELEVISION AIRTIME

Bill Clinton

In the following viewpoint, President Bill Clinton advocates free airtime for political candidates as part of his effort to reform campaign financing. He maintains that the United States is the only major democracy in which candidates need to raise increasingly large amounts of money to conduct successful campaigns. Free airtime will enhance the democratic process by allowing candidates to focus on issues instead of fund-raising and by lessening the influence of special interests, Clinton argues. He suggests that in exchange for providing free airtime, broadcasters should be given free rights to use digital technologies. These remarks were originally given at the Conference on Free TV and Political Reform in March 1997.

As you read, consider the following questions:

1. According to the author, what has been the major trend in campaign spending since 1972?
2. What does Clinton mean when he says that it is important to provide a "floor" for campaign spending?
3. How does the author believe skeptics will respond to his proposal? How does he answer the skeptics?

Excerpted from Bill Clinton's remarks to the Conference on Free TV and Political Reform, March 17, 1997.

Today we want to talk about whether the medium of free television could be used to diminish the impact of excessive money in politics and about whether it can be used, therefore, to reform our system in a way that makes it better and, ultimately, that leads to better decisions for the American people. It is now commonplace—everybody will tell you—that campaigns cost too much, and it takes too much time to raise the money, and the more money you raise from a larger number of people, the more questions will be raised about that.

Major party committees spent over 3 times as much in this last election cycle [1996] as 4 years before. And that doesn't count the third party expenditures, both the genuinely independent third party committees and those that weren't really independent although they claim to be. Spending in congressional campaigns has risen sixfold in the last two decades. That's over 3 times the rate of inflation. The biggest reason for this is the rise in the cost of television. But of course, there is also now more money being spent on mail, on telephoning, on radio, and on other print advertising as well.

In 1972, candidates spent $25 million for political ads; in 1996, $400 million. Presidential campaigns now routinely spend two-thirds or more of their money on paid ads; Senate candidates, 42 percent of their money on television; House races, about a third. Interestingly enough, that's often because there is no single television market which just overlaps a House district and often the cost is prohibitive, particularly in the urban districts. But you get the drift; it's the same everywhere.

We are the only major democracy in the world where candidates have to raise larger and larger sums of money simply to communicate with voters through the medium that matters most. Every other major democracy offers candidates or parties free air time to speak to voters, and we can plainly do better, building on the big first step urged by this group [the Conference on Free TV and Political Reform] in 1996. We have an obligation to restore our campaign finance system to a system that has the broad confidence of the American people but also of the American press that comments on it. In order to do that, television has to be part of the solution. I have said before and I will say again, everybody who has been involved in this system has to take responsibility for it and for changing it. . . .

PURSUING CAMPAIGN FINANCE REFORM

Having the right kind of campaign finance reform system and having the right kind of straight talk on television and having elections be more issue-oriented and having the debates of both sides heard clearly by all people and increasing voter interest and voter turnout, all these things will increase the likelihood that this laundry list of good things will be done and will be done in better fashion than would otherwise be the case. I think it is very important that those of you who care about this make this connection because that's how to build broad and deep support for this endeavor.

It seems to me that we do have an historic opportunity to pass campaign finance reform. And I think the public owes a lot of gratitude to Senator John McCain and Senator Russell Feingold and Congressman Christopher Shays and Congressman Martin Meehan and all of their supporters for the legislation they have offered. It is real and tough. It would level the playing field and reduce the role of big money in politics. It would set voluntary limits on campaign spending and ban soft money, all corporate contributions, and the very large individual ones. It would restrict the role of political action committees and lobbyists and make needed reforms within the confines of the Constitution as defined by existing Supreme Court case law.

PROVIDING A FLOOR

In all these ways, it would set ceilings on money in politics, and just as important, it would also provide a floor. And I think that is very important—it would also provide a floor. You actually have some Members in Congress who come from districts where there's a very low per capita income, for example, who are very afraid of campaign finance reform because they're afraid, among their own constituents, they'll never be able to raise enough money in their district to compete the first time a multimillionaire runs against them.

So the law has to give a floor. And McCain-Feingold does that by giving candidates free air time to talk directly to the voters if they observe the spending limits of the law. And we need to emphasize that any ceiling law should have a floor to guarantee that people have their say and are heard. It gives candidates deeply discounted rates for the purchase of time if they observe the limits of the law. In all these ways, it will level the playing field, giving new voices a chance to be heard and being fair to both parties.

I have supported the idea of free TV time for many years. When the Vice President was in Congress, he actually introduced legislation to require it. It was first proposed by President Kennedy in 1962. It has been around long enough. We now tried it in the last election more than ever before, and we know that it advances the public interest.

In my State of the Union Address, I asked Congress to pass the McCain-Feingold bill by July 4th, the day we celebrate the birth of our democracy. I pledge to you that I will continue to work with members of both parties to do this. I will be mustering more support out in the country . . . for this endeavor.

REQUIRING CANDIDATES TO APPEAR

The trouble with political advertising is that rival candidates don't have a mutual interest in expanding the market. They only want one more "customer" than the other guy. In a cynical time, the way to do that is not to grow your share, but to shrink his.

One way to break that dynamic is to require that candidates appear on screen—easy to do if the airtime is given free, probably unconstitutional under any other circumstances. If they can't hide behind faceless voices and clever pictures, candidates will be less quick with smears and distortions.

Paul Taylor, *Advertising Age*, April 28, 1997.

We have to use the present intense interest in this, as well as the controversy over fundraising in the last election and all the publicity on it, as a spur to action. We cannot let it become what it is in danger of becoming, which is an excuse for inaction.

And that again is something that I challenge all of you on. Do not let the controversy become an excuse to do nothing and to wallow around in it. Use it as a spur to changing the system, because until you change the system, you will continue to have controversies over the amount—the sheer amount—of money that is raised in these elections.

TRADING DIGITAL SIGNALS FOR FREE AIR TIME

The second thing I'd like to discuss . . . is how broadcasters can meet their public interest obligations in this era. Ever since the Federal Communications Commission (FCC) was created, broadcasters have had a compact with the public. In return for the public airwaves, they must meet public interest obligations. The bargain has been good for the industry and good for the public. Now, startling new technologies are shaking and remaking the world of telecommunications. They've opened wider opportunities for broadcasters than ever before, but they also offer us the chance to open wider vistas for our democracy as well.

The move from analog signals to digital ones will give each

broadcaster much more signal capacity than they have today. The broadcasters asked Congress to be given this new access to the public airwaves without charge. I believe, therefore, it is time to update broadcasters' public interest obligations to meet the demands of the new times and the new technological realities. I believe broadcasters who receive digital licenses should provide free air time for candidates, and I believe the FCC should act to require free air time for candidates.

LOOSENING THE GRIP OF BIG MONEY

The telecommunications revolution can help to transform our system so that once again voters have the loudest voice in our democracy. Free time for candidates can help free our democracy from the grip of big money. I hope all of you will support that. There are many ways that this could be done. Many of you here have put forward innovative plans. I believe the free time should be available to all qualified Federal candidates. I believe it should give candidates a chance to talk directly to the voters without gimmicks or intermediaries. Because campaign finance reform is so important, I believe it should be available especially to candidates who limit their own spending. It is clear under the Supreme Court decision that this can be done, and I believe that is how it should be done.

Candidates should be able to talk to voters based on the strength of their ideas, not the size of their pocketbooks, and all voters should know that no candidate is kept from running simply because he or she cannot raise enormous amounts of funds. . . .

OPENING AIRWAVES TO CANDIDATES

Finally, let me challenge the broadcasters as well. Broadcasters are not the problem, but broadcasting must be the solution. The step the broadcasters took in this last election, as I have said over and over again in other forums, with the encouragement of Straight Talk for TV, was a real breakthrough. Now I ask broadcasters to follow up on this experiment in democracy, and I'm especially pleased that a leader in the industry, Barry Diller, has challenged his colleagues to open up the airwaves to candidates. He has made clear, forcefully and very publicly, that he and all of his colleagues have an obligation to society, and his presence here today makes it clear that he is willing to assume the mantle of leadership. But surely there are others—I know there are— who will gladly join in and take up this cause as well.

There are many questions about political reform. Many skeptics will look at all proposed reform measures and ask whether

they'll work and whether there will be unintended consequences. The truth is that they will work and there will be unintended consequences.

But if we use that for an excuse not to change, no good
change in this country would ever have come about. There will
always be something we cannot foresee. That's what makes life
interesting and keeps us all humble, but that must not be an excuse for our refusing to act in this area. We know—we know—
when we work to expand our democracy, when you give people
a greater voice and advocates of all political views a firm platform upon which to stand, we are moving forward as a nation.
By passing campaign finance reform, by renewing the compact
between broadcasters and the public to better serve in this new
era, we can do that again.

And I will say again, I will do all I can on both these fronts, on
campaign finance reform legislation and on requiring free use,
free availability of the airwaves to public candidates. We need
your support for both, and we need broader and more intense
public support. And again I say, that has to be built by demon-
strating to the public that this is not an inside-the-beltway exercise in both parties trying to find ways to undermine each other
but a necessary way of opening our democracy so that we can
better, more quickly, and more profoundly address the real chal-
lenges facing the American people in their everyday lives. These
two steps will help, and together I hope we can make them.

> "Broadcasters have a great tradition
> of voluntarily offering free time for
> debates. The dirty little secret is that
> politicians have an equally long
> tradition of rejecting those offers."

POLITICAL CANDIDATES SHOULD NOT RECEIVE FREE TELEVISION AIRTIME

Edward O. Fritts

In the following viewpoint, Edward O. Fritts argues that television broadcasters should not be required to give political candidates free airtime. According to the author, candidates already receive extensive airtime in the form of debates and news coverage. Further, he cites studies showing that candidates do not use all the free airtime that they are currently offered. Edward O. Fritts is president and CEO of the National Association of Broadcasters.

As you read, consider the following questions:

1. According to the author, what did Dwight Morris's study of the 1990 and 1994 political campaigns reveal about rising campaign costs?
2. What does this viewpoint reveal about the March 12, 1996, Wisconsin primary debates?
3. What does Fritts conclude about the constitutionality of publicly funded campaigns?

Reprinted from Edward O. Fritts, "Free TV Time for Candidates?" *Campaigns and Elections*, December 1997, by permission.

If campaign finance reform is the answer, what is the question? That's the current debate, and there are those who think they have it all figured out: mandate more free television airtime for candidates.

Conventional wisdom holds that the cost of communicating has risen so dramatically that candidates are forced to raise huge sums of money just to remain competitive. Give politicians more free TV time, costs will drop, and presto! . . . the campaign finance system will be reformed!

As usual, the conventional wisdom is flat wrong. Just ask Dwight Morris, the former *Los Angeles Times* reporter who now runs the Campaign Study Group. Morris studied more than 1,400 House and Senate races waged between '90 and '94. His conclusion: "despite a mountain of readily available evidence to the contrary, most journalists and Sunday morning talking heads desperately cling to the notion that television advertising is the primary culprit behind ever-rising campaign costs." Journalists, said Morris, "have been misleading the public for years."

CARPET BOMBING THE ELECTORATE

The cost of individual TV ads is not the reason why campaign costs have soared. Candidates, through their consultants, are simply buying more time each year—three times as much as was purchased 10 years ago—in an effort to "carpet bomb" the electorate with more attack ads.

Broadcasters would like to see the level of political discourse enhanced, as evidenced by the thousands of hours of free time each election season in the form of news coverage, candidate profiles, public affairs programming and debates. That's the type of coverage valued by the American people, rather than a federally-mandated free time plan that would simply enable politicians to double up on negative attack ads.

Legitimate campaign coverage—the kind of free time that is freely given by broadcasters—is indeed what voters desire. Opinion Research Corp. polled voters in April 1997 on behalf of PROMAX and asked what TV format provided the most valuable candidate information. The results: 36% chose debates; 30% chose newscasts; 17% chose public affairs and interview programs; 6% chose political advertising and 11% had no comment/no response.

In other words, 83 percent of respondents said they received their most valuable information from free airtime already donated by broadcasters. Moreover, 61 percent of those surveyed opposed giving politicians free airtime on top of existing paid advertising.

REJECTING OFFERS

Broadcasters have a great tradition of voluntarily offering free time for debates. The dirty little secret is that politicians have an equally long tradition of rejecting those offers.

Examples:

• WRC-TV in Washington, D.C. went to great lengths to schedule an Oct. 29, 1997, Virginia gubernatorial debate between major candidates. The 30-minute, commercial-free debate would have aired on the NBC affiliate at 7:30 p.m. a week before the election. One of the major candidates declined the offer, even after contending he could not buy all the ad time he was seeking.

• As reported in *National Journal*, Wisconsin Broadcasting Association President John Laabs "routinely sponsors senatorial and gubernatorial debates." In 1996, Laabs went a step further, orchestrating a multi-state debate between the GOP presidential hopefuls on the eve of Wisconsin's March 12 primary. Primaries were slated all over the country that month, so Laabs won the cooperation of broadcast associations in 12 other states, with dozens of television stations agreeing to run the program live. The value of the debate time was in the millions of dollars. But there was a catch: the candidates never showed.

• President Clinton, a free time advocate, along with Senator Dole, each declined 30 minutes of free time offered on election eve in '96 by the Fox network. There were no strings attached, no moderators and no spin doctors. Yet the no-cost offered time was rejected.

ADHERING TO PUBLIC INTEREST

If the politicians are really concerned about the public interest, perhaps they should ask the American public if it wants free political advertising on TV. Wonder how that would turn out. Generally speaking, what's in the interest of politicians is not in the public interest at all.

W.F. Gloede, *Mediaweek*, October 27, 1997.

Let's also note that federal law already requires TV stations to provide candidates "lowest unit rate" advertising that is equivalent to about a 30 percent discount. That break translates into millions in savings for candidates in each election.

AN UNCONSTITUTIONAL MANDATE

Advocates of federally-mandated free time argue that since broadcasters use the public airwaves, the public would benefit by defraying the cost of campaigning. But FCC member Rachelle Chong parries that argument quite succinctly. "If you follow this line of reasoning," says Chong, "maybe we should ask airlines to give free airplane seats to political candidates—airlines use the public airways . . . too!"

Finally, Sen. Arlen Specter (R-PA) makes the valid point that a free airtime mandate is unconstitutional in that it violates the Fifth Amendment standard on taking property without due process of law.

Our system of community-based broadcasting—founded on a commitment to localism and the First Amendment—continues to serve audiences and voters across the country. The public makes clear it values debates, candidate profiles and public affairs programs most, and more political ads least. Broadcasters are explicitly fulfilling the public's desire.

PERIODICAL BIBLIOGRAPHY

The following articles have been selected to supplement the diverse views presented in this chapter. Addresses are provided for periodicals not indexed in the *Readers' Guide to Periodical Literature*, the *Alternative Press Index*, the *Social Sciences Index*, or the *Index to Legal Periodicals and Books*.

David Awbrey	"Liberal Bias Isn't the Problem, Cultural Bias Is," *American Editor*, July/August 1996. Available from 11690 Sunrise Valley Dr., No. B, Reston, VA 20191.
Thad Beyle, Donald Ostdiek, and G. Patrick Lynch	"Is the State Press Corps Biased? The View from Political and Media Elites," *Spectrum*, Fall 1996.
James Boylan	"Punishing the Press: The Public Passes Some Tough Judgements on Libel, Fairness, and 'Fraud,'" *Columbia Journalism Review*, March/April 1997.
Everette E. Dennis	"Liberal Reporters, Yes; Liberal Slant, No!" *American Editor*, January/February 1997.
Bernadette C. Hayes and Toni Makkai	"Politics and the Mass Media: The Differential Impact of Gender," *Women & Politics*, Fall 1996.
Joel Kotkin and David Friedman	"Clueless: Why the Elite Media Don't Understand America," *American Enterprise*, March/April 1998.
Mark Crispin Miller	"Free the Media," *Nation*, June 1996.
Michael Parenti	"Methods of Media Manipulation," *Humanist*, July/August 1997.
Susan Paterino	"The Intervention Dilemma," *American Journalism Review*, March 1998.
Thomas E. Patterson	"Time and News: The Media's Limitations as an Instrument of Democracy," *International Political Science Review*, January 1998.
Quill	"Making the Tough Decisions," January/February 1997. Available from 16 S. Jackson St., Greencastle, IN 46135-1514.
Carl Sessions Stepp	"The Fallout from Too Much Crime Coverage," *American Journalism Review*, April 1998.

John H. Summers	"Journalists or Defenders of the Faith?" *Free Inquiry*, Spring 1998. Available from Box 664, Buffalo, NY 14226.
Rebecca Tallent	"New Ethics Code Not to Restrain, but Minimize Harm; Without Trust," *Quill*, January/February 1997.
Gore Vidal	"The End of History," *Nation*, September 30, 1996.
David Wagner	"Making News, Breaking Ethics," *Insight*, March 1997. Available from 3600 New York Ave. NE, Washington, DC 20002.

CHAPTER 4

SHOULD PORNOGRAPHY ON THE INTERNET BE REGULATED?

Chapter Preface

Internet use has grown exponentially since the network's creation in the late 1960s. Originally conceived as a way to connect major research institutions, the Internet has become one of the world's major communications media. In 1989, British computer scientist Timothy Berners-Lee created the World Wide Web to link scientific research sites in all parts of the world. By the early 1990s, the World Wide Web, also called the WWW or W3, had become a mainstay of Internet users everywhere. According to the Internet consulting company Nua, by 1996 the Web was being used by 45 million people worldwide and by 30 million people in North America.

With this increase in use, and with powerful search engines capable of accessing vast stores of information, many people have become concerned by the ease with which children can access information deemed objectionable, including pornography. In 1996, responding to this concern, Congress passed the Communications Decency Act (CDA) as part of the Telecommunications Act. The CDA was designed to protect minors from accessing indecent material, including pornography, over the Internet. However, in 1997, the Supreme Court ruled the CDA unconstitutional because it violated the First Amendment right to free speech.

Since then, proponents of regulation have struggled to find ways to protect children from accidentally encountering pornography on the Internet. For instance, some advocate equipping libraries with filtering software to block out offensive sites. Others promote self-regulating systems that require Internet service providers to rate themselves. Stephen Balkam, the executive director of the Recreational Software Advisory Council, writes that "with the right framework, checks and balances, oversight and controls, self-regulation is by far a more attractive route to take than central government mandate."

Both of these plans have come under attack from free-speech advocates such as the American Library Association and the American Civil Liberties Union. These organizations believe that outside regulation of Internet sites will have a chilling effect on free speech because it will limit open discussion of controversial topics such as birth control, abortion, homosexuality, and AIDS. For instance, Thomas W. Hazlett and David W. Sosa of the University of California, Davis, write that "content regulation lends itself to abuse by political interest groups and thereby imposes sharp disincentives on those who would air controversial opinions."

In the absence of any sure way to protect children from Internet pornography and promote free speech, policy makers must weigh the relative merits of protection and freedom. The viewpoints in this chapter debate the best way to keep the Internet free and safe.

"If the Founding Fathers had lived in an age of Internet, they might have reworded the First Amendment."

INTERNET PORNOGRAPHY SHOULD BE REGULATED

William F. Buckley Jr.

As part of the Telecommunications Act of 1996, Congress passed a provision known as the Communications Decency Act (CDA), which was designed to protect children from pornography on the Internet. In 1997 the Supreme Court ruled the CDA unconstitutional. In the following viewpoint, William F. Buckley Jr. argues that the Supreme Court made a serious mistake in overturning the CDA. He believes that, although the Internet is an important technological tool, pornography on the Internet is harmful and should be kept out of the reach of children. Buckley is the founder and editor of *National Review*, a conservative journal.

As you read, consider the following questions:

1. On what basis does Buckley oppose Justice Stevens's opinion that the Internet will do more good than harm?
2. What does the author mean by the "utilitarian argument"?
3. What are the shortcomings of devices that block offensive Internet content, according to Buckley?

The Supreme Court decision on the Internet and pornography is analytically infuriating. Justice John Paul Stevens used as the principal argument for the majority opinion invalidating the congressional act the assertion that the Internet is going to do more good than harm. He went so far in this line of argument as to say that such harm as it does is unmeasured and perhaps impalpable—the old argument: Who ever got hurt by pornography? But to argue that more good than harm can come from the Internet is on the order of saying that more good than harm can come from drugs and therefore commerce in prussic acid should not be forbidden.

MAKING A CONSTITUTIONAL ARGUMENT

My own judgment of the Internet is that it is the most exciting technological research and information tool of the twentieth century, but this has nothing at all to do with the challenge of ensuring that only adults would have access to its darker corners. If Mr. Justice Stevens had said simply that there probably isn't any way to keep porn off teenage screens, he'd have been persuasive—letting the case rest on that utilitarian point. We know it wasn't possible to keep liquor outside national boundaries, and every day we learn what are the sacrifices necessary to make it hard for sub-intelligent people to buy marijuana—moderately resourceful people have no problem.

But of course the Court had to accost the legal question, Was the Communications Decency Act constitutional? Ever since its passage in early 1996 it was expected that the Act would be shot down quickly by the courts, as indeed it was, first by the D.C. Court of Appeals, now by the Supreme Court. But the question is left open: Is this a matter of defective constitutional architecture, or do we have a circle-squaring problem? Is it simply impossible? "I don't think some members of Congress have ever read the Constitution," said Rep. Anna Eshoo of California. Her insight is interesting. But it invites the comment that if the Founding Fathers had lived in an age of Internet, they might have reworded the First Amendment.

TAKING ON THE UTILITARIAN ARGUMENT

The utilitarian argument is the one to take on, and it isn't easy. There are devices for the Internet similar to those being attempted to bar porn from television screens. One system would block twenty thousand websites, another would authorize only three thousand, and both would require weekly adjustments to compensate for the ingenuity of young porn-seekers. "Right now," comments Mariam Bell, the vice president of Enough Is Enough, an anti-pornography group, "it's like a defective condom." One might add as relevant here that any 13-year-old can go to any magazine stand or bookstore and pull up anything (I am assuming) that the Internet can give him. The public has the satisfaction of vague laws that classify movies and push television pornography up from kiddie-time to 8 P.M., mildly inconveniencing 10-year-olds. But the local VHS store makes available stuff that would have soothed the Marquis de Sade. The public will to protest the crowning of King Porn ended when the Supreme Court's decision to okay Deep Throat went substantially unprotested.

David Kalish of the Associated Press suggests the frustration of parents who have experienced the technical problem of diverting unwanted material. "Type in the word 'toy' on the popular AltaVista site-search engine and the second choice that blinks up isn't GI Joe or Barbie. It's the Nice N Naughty Adult Toy Store, hawking the Felicia Fantasy Doll, the Testicular Stimulator, and the Precision Power Pump."

Sex is a powerful stimulant to the curiosity and to the masturbatory human inclination. The *Washington Post*'s Rajiv Chandrasekaran and Elizabeth Corcoran write nicely on the evolution of the Internet. The fable of the sorcerer's apprentice comes to mind. But here Justice Stevens correctly remarks, however irrelevantly, that more good is going to come from the Internet than non-good. If the printing press hadn't evolved, *Mein Kampf* would have had to be hand-copied, but so too Shakespeare. The *Post's* story notes, "When Defense Department researchers wired together a set of university computers 31 years ago, creating a communications network that became today's global Internet, the goal was not to make something that could deliver photos from a service called . . ."—but I'll put it in Pig Latin: to discourage the kids—Iancabay's Mutsay Hacksay.

Parents who care will of course encourage and patronize the blocking devices. But in the back of their minds they will know that this fight, on this front, is lost.

"The CDA was a cruel blunt
instrument meant to further the
political agenda of a self-absorbed
'chosen few' that deemed themselves
the guardians of our children and
purveyors of All-American good taste."

INTERNET PORNOGRAPHY SHOULD NOT BE REGULATED

Brock N. Meeks

In the following viewpoint, Brock N. Meeks argues that the Communications Decency Act (CDA), passed by Congress in 1996 as part of the Telecommunications Act and struck down by the Supreme Court the following year, was too vague and broad to effectively control pornography on the Internet. He claims that the act would have restricted free speech by equating the terms "obscenity," which implies sexually graphic material, and "indecency," which is much more broadly defined and includes anything that anyone deems offensive. Therefore, according to Meeks, the law would have forced legitimate Internet journalists to censor their speech in order to avoid negative repercussions. Further, it would have threatened other types of free speech, such as discussions of birth control and homosexuality. Meeks is the chief Washington correspondent for MSNBC on the Internet.

As you read, consider the following questions:

1. How would the CDA have affected parental choices, according to Meeks?
2. How did the Supreme Court respond to the charge that children could discover pornography on the Internet accidentally, as cited by Meeks?

Reprinted from Brock N. Meeks, "Communications Decency Act: Debating (What Once Was) the CDA," *Communications of the ACM*, September 1997, by permission of the author.

I must be living right. First, my net-based publication Cyber-Wire Dispatch was one of the plaintiffs that challenged the Communications Decency Act (CDA) as unconstitutional, eventually winning the case before the U.S. Supreme Court. Second, being asked to write this Viewpoint. Giving my thoughts on the case is a no-brainer: the Court's stinging denouncement of the CDA serves as a legal cheat sheet.

In other words, I'm on the side of angels.

Right from jump street, the Court left no doubt as to the unconstitutional nature of the CDA. Justice John Paul Stevens, writing for the majority, says: "As a matter of constitutional tradition, in the absence of evidence to the contrary, we presume that governmental regulation of the content of speech is more likely to interfere with the free exchange of ideas than to encourage it. The interest in encouraging freedom of expression in a democratic society outweighs any theoretical but unproven benefit of censorship."

The key phrase there is "theoretical but unproven benefit of censorship." Let's get one thing cleared up right away. The CDA was never, ever about pornography or "smut" on the Internet, despite what 95% of all newspaper headlines inferred. Instead, the CDA was a cruel blunt instrument meant to further the political agenda of a self-absorbed "chosen few" that deemed themselves the guardians of our children and purveyors of All-American good taste. No, scratch that. The supporters of the CDA deemed themselves the guardians of my and your children.

THE ISSUE OF PARENTAL CHOICE

Indeed, this issue of parental choice was one of the stalwart levers the Court pulled to make its case. Nowhere in the CDA were there provisions for parents to decide what their kids could or couldn't see. Suppose I believe my 16-year-old son is mature enough to handle erotic literature? If the CDA were now law, I could be thrown in jail and guilty of a felony if I "knowingly" allowed my son to read erotic stories on the Internet.

Although the justices split on one provision of the CDA in a 7-2 vote, they were unanimous in saying that the law was vague and overbroad. The Court's decision called the CDA "a content-based blanket restriction on speech." After reading that, you have to ask: What part of that sentence don't the misguided supporters of the CDA understand?

The Court was rightly concerned the CDA would have a profound negative impact on important, critical areas of speech such as "birth control practices, homosexuality," and "the consequences of prison rape," not to mention Gonzo journalism as practiced by me on the Internet. In addition, the harsh and criminal nature of the penalties attached to this law "may well cause speakers to remain silent rather than communicate even arguably unlawful words, ideas and images," the Court said.

A Linguistic Shell Game

Next, the Court saw right through the linguistic shell game the CDA supporters tried to pull in attempting to conflate the meaning of "obscenity" with "indecency." The Court said, "each of the two parts of the CDA uses a different linguistic form," one mentioning "obscenity" and the other "indecency."

During the U.S. Federal District Court proceedings in Philadelphia, where the CDA was first slam-dunked before heading to the Supreme Court, the Justice Department lawyers defending the CDA admitted flat out, under cross-examination by the three-judge panel in Philadelphia, that, yes, the law did equate "indecency" with "obscenity." If not for the extreme decorum of the district court judges, they might have broken out into laughter at this remark. In fact, rumor has it that over brandy and a few Cuban cigars after that hearing in judges' chambers, this is exactly what took place.

STANDING UP FOR FREE SPEECH

Just as we had become used to our freedoms being worn away, a federal court did the right thing. It stood up for the right to free speech by declaring unconstitutional parts of the Communications Decency Act, which gave Washington power to regulate the Internet.

We didn't have to wait for this decision to know that government's attempt to clean up the Internet would ultimately fail. The law is unnecessary and unworkable, a threat to a medium that has thus far served the public extremely well. It comes with no viable plan for shielding children, other than granting new powers to government bureaucrats. . . .

The cry "We must protect the children" has been responsible for the many abuses of the welfare state. It is an easy sell when someone wants to grab power. When politicians say they want to regulate the Internet for the same reason, think twice.

Robert A. Sirico, *Forbes*, July 29, 1996.

Under provisions of the now-defunct CDA, I would have had to write my CyberWire Dispatch (CWD) as if the most prudish, blue-nose community in the nation were watching over my shoulder, ready to rap my knuckles any time I used a four-letter word. This is known in Judicial circles as the "Heckler's Veto," where a single person's complaint can squash an idea, or in this case, speech.

The Supreme Court realized this in saying: "[A]ny opponent of indecent speech . . . might simply log on and inform the would-be discoursers that his 17-year-old child . . . would be present." If this had happened, under provisions of the CDA that said if I "knowingly" transmitted "indecent" speech to a minor, I would either have to withdraw my Internet column or send it into cyberspace, "knowing" that I was committing a crime. Or settle for another option: write CWD with all the intellectual heft of a Barney the Dinosaur script.

The Court also laid to rest the bogeyman that kids could stumble unwittingly across smut on the Internet. For this to be true, the net would have to be pervasive. But the Court, rightly, didn't see it that way. The decision says: "Though [indecent] material is widely available, users rarely encounter such content accidentally . . . the odds are slim that a user would enter a sexually explicit site by accident." And unlike TV or radio, anyone using the net must purposefully take "a series of affirmative steps more deliberate and directed than merely turning a dial" to find smut.

WASTING THE TAXPAYERS' MONEY

Perhaps the most gratifying development that came about through this huge waste of taxpayer money (the cost to try the case) is that the Court codified the unique nature and culture of the Internet. The Court realized the medium of cyberspace is a publishing environment like none we've ever seen. Justice Stevens pulled a kind of "back to the future" move when he paraphrased the 40-year-old anti-censorship Supreme Court decision in *Butler vs. Michigan*, which said restricting speech is like "burning down the house to roast the pig," when he wrote: "[t]he CDA, casting a far darker shadow over free speech, threatens to torch a large segment of the Internet community."

Amen and amen.

> "The use of filtering software by libraries to block access to constitutionally protected speech violates the Library Bill of Rights."

LIBRARIES SHOULD NOT REGULATE INTERNET ACCESS

American Library Association Intellectual Freedom Committee

The American Library Association (ALA), founded in 1876, is the oldest and largest library association in the world. In the following viewpoint, the ALA's Intellectual Freedom Committee argues that libraries need to maintain the freedom to provide unfettered Internet access to all patrons. To accomplish this goal, it believes it imperative to avoid using filtering software to block users' access to pornographic websites. The ALA contends that such software blocks not only material that some people consider "offensive," but also sites that provide useful information on subjects such as breast cancer, AIDS, women's rights, and animal rights.

As you read, consider the following questions:

1. What are the five types of filtering software listed by the ALA?
2. What are some of the problems with filtering software, as described by the ALA?
3. What is the responsibility of parents regarding their children's use of the Internet, according to the ALA?

Reprinted by permission of the American Library Association from its Intellectual Freedom Committee's "Statement on Library Use of Filtering Software," July 1, 1997.

On June 26, 1997, the United States Supreme Court issued a sweeping re-affirmation of core First Amendment principles and held that communications over the Internet deserve the highest level of Constitutional protection.

The Court's most fundamental holding is that communications on the Internet deserve the same level of Constitutional protection as books, magazines, newspapers, and speakers on a street corner soapbox. The Court found that the Internet "constitutes a vast platform from which to address and hear from a world-wide audience of millions of readers, viewers, researchers, and buyers," and that "any person with a phone line can become a town crier with a voice that resonates farther than it could from any soapbox."

For libraries, the most critical holding of the Supreme Court is that libraries that make content available on the Internet can continue to do so with the same Constitutional protections that apply to the books on libraries' shelves. The Court's conclusion that "the vast democratic fora of the Internet" merit full constitutional protection will also serve to protect libraries that provide their patrons with access to the Internet. The Court recognized the importance of enabling individuals to receive speech from the entire world and to speak to the entire world. Libraries provide those opportunities to many who would not otherwise have them. The Supreme Court's decision will protect that access.

The use in libraries of software filters which block Constitutionally protected speech is inconsistent with the United States Constitution and federal law and may lead to legal exposure for the library and its governing authorities. The American Library Association affirms that the use of filtering software by libraries to block access to constitutionally protected speech violates the Library Bill of Rights.

WHAT IS BLOCKING/FILTERING SOFTWARE?

Blocking/filtering software is a mechanism used to:
- restrict access to Internet content, based on an internal database of the product, or;
- restrict access to Internet content through a database maintained external to the product itself, or;
- restrict access to Internet content to certain ratings assigned to those sites by a third party, or;
- restrict access to Internet content by scanning content, based on a keyword, phrase or text string or;
- restrict access to Internet content based on the source of the information.

Problems with Blocking/Filtering Software in Libraries

Publicly supported libraries are governmental institutions subject to the First Amendment, which forbids them from restricting information based on viewpoint or content discrimination.

Libraries are places of inclusion rather than exclusion. Current blocking/filtering software prevents not only access to what some may consider "objectionable" material, but also blocks information protected by the First Amendment. The result is that legal and useful material will inevitably be blocked. Examples of sites that have been blocked by popular commercial blocking/filtering products include those on breast cancer, AIDS, women's rights, and animal rights.

Filters can impose the producer's viewpoint on the community.

Producers do not generally reveal what is being blocked, or provide methods for users to reach sites that were inadvertently blocked.

Criteria used to block content are vaguely defined and subjectively applied.

The vast majority of Internet sites are informative and useful. Blocking/filtering software often blocks access to materials it is not designed to block.

Most blocking/filtering software is designed for the home market. Filters are intended to respond to the preferences of parents making decisions for their own children. Libraries are responsible for serving a broad and diverse community with different preferences and views. Blocking Internet sites is antithetical to library missions because it requires the library to limit information access.

In a library setting, filtering today is a one-size-fits-all "solution," which cannot adapt to the varying ages and maturity levels of individual users.

A role of librarians is to advise and assist users in selecting information resources. Parents and only parents have the right and responsibility to restrict their own children's access—and only their own children's access—to library resources, including the Internet. Librarians do not serve in loco parentis.

Library use of blocking/filtering software creates an implied contract with parents that their children will not be able to access material on the Internet that they do not wish their children to read or view. Libraries will be unable to fulfill this implied contract, due to the technological limitations of the software, thus exposing themselves to possible legal liability and litigation.

Laws prohibiting the production or distribution of child pornography and obscenity apply to the Internet. These laws provide protection for libraries and their users.

How Can You and Your Library Promote Access to the Internet?

Educate yourself, your staff, library board, governing bodies, community leaders, parents, elected officials, etc., about the Internet and how best to take advantage of the wealth of information available. . . .

Uphold the First Amendment by establishing and implementing written guidelines and policies on Internet use in your library in keeping with your library's overall policies on access to library materials. . . .

Unfriendly Filters

In order to determine the impact of software filters on the open exchange of information on the Internet, the Electronic Privacy Information Center conducted 100 searches using a traditional search engine and then conducted the same 100 searches using a new search engine that is advertised as the "world's first family-friendly Internet search site." We tried to locate information about 25 schools; 25 charitable and political organizations; 25 educational, artistic, and cultural institutions; and 25 concepts that might be of interest to young people. Our search terms included such phrases as the "American Red Cross," the "San Diego Zoo," and the "Smithsonian Institution," as well as such concepts as "Christianity," the "Bill of Rights" and "eating disorders." In every case in our sample, we found that the family-friendly search engine prevented us from obtaining access to almost 90 percent of the materials on the Internet containing the relevant search terms. We further found that in many cases, the search service denied access to 99 percent of material that would otherwise be available without the filters. We concluded that the filtering mechanism prevented children from obtaining a great deal of useful and appropriate information that is currently available on the Internet.

Electronic Privacy Information Center, "Faulty Filters: How Content Filters Block Access to Kid-Friendly Information on the Internet," December 1997.

Promote Internet use by facilitating user access to Web sites that satisfy user interest and needs.

Create and promote library Web pages designed both for general use and for use by children. These pages should point to sites that have been reviewed by library staff.

Consider using privacy screens or arranging terminals away from public view to protect a user's confidentiality.

Provide information and training for parents and minors that remind users of time, place and manner restrictions on Internet use.

Establish and implement user behavior policies.

| "When a library allows everything on the Internet, it already has imposed a set of values on the community: the values of free speech absolutism."

LIBRARIES SHOULD REGULATE INTERNET ACCESS

David Burt

In the following viewpoint, David Burt responds to the American Library Association's (ALA) opposition to the use of Internet filtering/blocking software in libraries. He argues that such software targets only a small number of websites, most of which are pornographic and therefore inappropriate for library patrons. In addition, he asserts that filtering pornographic sites is consistent with the policies of libraries across the country to omit pornographic magazines and videos from their collections. Libraries must take responsibility for their part in raising children, he contends, and that means finding ways to keep them from accessing offensive materials. Burt is president and founder of Filtering Facts, a nonprofit organization that promotes the use of filtering software in libraries.

As you read, consider the following questions:

1. What does the author mean by "collateral damage"? What evidence does he provide that such damage will be minimal?
2. What did Burt's survey reveal about libraries that have used filtering devices?
3. How does the author respond to the assertion by the ALA that filtering will hand over control of libraries to nonlibrarians?

Reprinted from David Burt, "Statement of Filtering Facts in Response to the American Library Association Statement to the Senate Commerce, Science, and Transportation Committee on Indecency on the Internet," March 7, 1998, by permission of the author. Available at www.filteringfacts.org/mccain.htm.

During the debate over filtering in libraries, the American Library Association (ALA) has often exhibited what could only be called an extreme stand on the free speech rights of children. ALA President-elect Ann Symons, in a 1997 interview with *Wired*, was asked if a 13-year-old wanted to obtain pornography, would she in any way stand in the child's way? Symons' response was "I would say from my point of view there shouldn't be, and if the library didn't own this material and you as a 13-year-old asked for an interlibrary loan, that should be granted to you just as it would an adult patron." ALA's acknowledged "point person" on the filtering issue, ALA Office of Intellectual Freedom director Judith Krug, has denied that a problem with children accessing pornography even exists. Krug recently said "their number is so small that it is almost laughable," and "only one child out of a trillion billion" might use library computers to seek out pornography. When asked if even the display of bestiality in a library might be problematic, Krug answered that "Blocking material leads to censorship. That goes for pornography and bestiality, too. If you don't like it, don't look at it."

Assessing Collateral Damage

The ALA statement argues that "the use of blocking software deprives the community of access to many sites that provide valuable as well as constitutionally protected information for both adults and children on subjects ranging from AIDS and breast cancer to religion and politics." While it is acknowledged that filters are imperfect, the best evidence suggests that the amount of "collateral damage" done to innocent speech is trivial.

It is estimated that pornography sites represent only a small portion of the Internet. Estimates usually range from 1 to 3% of all the Internet web sites. The pornography filters are only aiming at this small portion of 1 to 3% of the Internet, and the "blacklists" of banned web sites the filters use only contain 30,000 to 100,000 sites.

It is not known what percentage of the filtering companies' "blacklists" are non-pornographic sites, but based on incidents where "hacker" vigilantes have decrypted the blacklists of products such as X-Stop, SurfWatch, and CyberPatrol, the best evidence is that the number of "bad blocks" in the blacklists of these filters is very small. After "cleaning up" the X-Stop database, the company CEO reported about 300 bad blocks, or about .5% of the total blacklist. After a group calling itself "The Censorware Project" decrypted CyberPatrol's list, they found about 60 bad blocks, or about .1% of the total blacklist. A few dozen or a few hundred bad blocks is only a tiny fraction of 1% of the entire Internet. Since the number of these bad blocks is very small, we would expect to see a very small number of complaints about them in libraries.

In 1997, I surveyed 24 public library administrators who filtered and asked them how many complaints they received about inappropriately blocked sites. The average number was 1.6 per month, with 71% receiving one or less complaint each month. Seven of the libraries reported never receiving a single complaint. These libraries have an easy way to overcome the minor deficiencies of filtering software, which is to have the librarian override the filter for a patron who encounters an inappropriately blocked site.

Without further study, such as a direct monitoring of patron behavior while using a filtered Internet terminal, we cannot say what the true amount of "collateral damage" is to innocent speech. Yet we can say that the evidence seems to be pointing in a particular direction, and that is that filters do not significantly interfere with library patron access to legitimate information.

FILTERING PORNOGRAPHIC MAGAZINES AND VIDEOS

The ALA statement says that, "while blocking and filtering products can be useful tools for parents to use at home, their use in a library setting is questionable at best. Libraries serve all the families and all library users in a given community. As public institutions supported primarily by local public tax monies, libraries are obligated to meet the information needs of the entire community or school population, while upholding the basic principles of the First Amendment."

It cannot be emphasized strongly enough that "filtering out" pornographic magazines and videos is the rule in libraries. While some public libraries do in fact carry a very small amount of "soft core" pornography such as *Playboy*, or explicit materials for artistic or educational purposes such as *The Joy of Sex* and Madonna's *Sex*, no public library in the United States carries what most reasonable persons would call "hard-core pornography." A quick survey of the most popular pornographic titles in the national library holdings database OCLC verifies this. Not one of the 8,921 public library systems in the United States subscribes to *Hustler* magazine. Nor does any public library own a copy of the video *Deep Throat*, *Behind the Green Door*, nor any other such title.

Pornography in the print and video formats are excluded from all public libraries by the conscious choice of librarians.

This is done intentionally for the obvious reason that pornography is not appropriate for an institution like a public library.

The ALA statement also claims that "when a library installs commercial filters or blocking software, it transfers the professional judgement about the information needs of the community from the librarian to anonymous third parties—often part time workers with no credentials and no ties to the community—who evaluate sites for the software 'manufacturer.'"

PROTECTING CHILDREN FROM SEXUAL PREDATORS

We are talking about protecting children from sexual predators who have found in the Internet a way to peddle their wares around the globe. We don't place books advocating bestiality and pedophilia on the shelves of the local library; why tolerate them on the library's computer?

Lars-Erik Nelson, *Liberal Opinion*, December 15, 1997.

It is true that filtering involves turning over some of the selection of materials to non-librarians. This is nothing new to libraries. Librarians have relied on vendors to pre-select for them for years. Buying books on an approval plan or buying full-text magazines on a CD-ROM also involves letting a vendor do a certain amount of selection for the librarian. There is nothing inherently immoral or unethical with this type of "outsourcing" of selection. In fact, as the bibliographic universe becomes ever larger, turning over portions of selection duties to outside vendors has become a necessity for most libraries.

PRESERVING A FLOOR OF APPROPRIATENESS

The ALA statement says that "children must learn to handle and reject content that may be offensive to their values and to adhere to online safety rules when confronted with uncomfortable situations." This implies a belief that the exposure of children to pornography is probably inevitable, and that children should be prepared for such exposure, rather than shielded from it. In many communities, children were protected from pornography until unfiltered Internet access was provided to them by their local public libraries. The ALA statement argues that this unwelcome change to communities should not be reversed. Filtering Facts could not disagree more strongly. A library would not purchase *Hustler*, then place it next to *Hi-lights* in the children's room, then offer a special class to teach children how to decide not to look at it.

The ALA often charges that filtering involves imposing someone else's values upon all children. When a library allows everything on the Internet, it already has imposed a set of values on the community: the values of free speech absolutism. All that we are asking is that libraries exclude from children materials on the Internet that they would never acquire for children in print or video formats. Filtering attempts to preserve the same "floor" of appropriateness that already exists de facto in every public library in the United States. Providing unfiltered Internet access to children rips up this "floor" and imposes an agenda of free speech absolutism upon libraries and communities that did not ask for such a new standard and do not want it.

It does take a village to raise a child, and the library is part of that village. When parents live in a community where their children are protected from pornography, they have a right to ask that the library assist them in making the library a safe place for children to learn and to enjoy. That really isn't asking that much.

"The ultimate goal of [rating] systems is to provide a technical alternative to government regulation and censorship."

SELF-RATING OF INTERNET SITES WILL NOT VIOLATE FREE SPEECH

C. Dianne Martin and Joseph M. Reagle Jr.

In the following viewpoint, C. Dianne Martin and Joseph M. Reagle Jr. demonstrate how Internet self-rating systems, also called content advisory systems, can provide useful information on sex and violence on websites without governmental censorship. They argue that a self-rating system can protect parents and children against unwanted and offensive intrusions while preserving the freedom of website creators. Martin is president of the Recreational Software Advisory Council (RSAC) and teaches at George Washington University. Reagle represents the World Wide Web Consortium (W3C) and teaches at Massachusetts Institute of Technology.

As you read, consider the following questions:

1. What is the difference between a rating system and a rating service, as described by the authors?
2. According to the authors, how might cultural bias play a role in rating systems?

Excerpted from C. Dianne Martin and Joseph M. Reagle Jr., "An Alternative to Government Regulation and Censorship: Content Advisory Systems for the Internet," Spring 1996, by permission of the authors. Available at www.rsac.org/fra_content.asp?onIndex=37.

With the huge increase of on-line users below the age of 18 caused by the explosive growth of on-line services and access in the United States and other technologically sophisticated nations, there has been an accompanying surge in the availability of adult oriented content and services that has generated much concern for the protection of the public and children, in particular, from exposure to inappropriate content. As a result, a plethora of government policies and industry strategies have been proposed for dealing with this social problem.

Due to the competing interests between government control and regulation of content on the one hand and the individual privacy, autonomy, and free speech on the other hand, several industry coalitions have been formed to develop and endorse voluntary content labeling and blocking systems that can be embedded in the very technologies creating the problem, thus providing technological alternatives to censorship and regulation of the Internet. . . .

The Recreational Software Advisory Council (RSAC) system is voluntary with specific deterministic [objective] criteria by which content is rated in a descriptive manner. Content producers, such as video game makers, answer a detailed questionnaire (either in paper or electronic format) about their content with respect to violence, nudity, sex, and language. RSAC then processes the questionnaire, registers and returns the consequent rating to the company. The company is able to use that label in advertising or on their product. The label consists of a number, between (0–4), for each of the four categories. A rating of All (0) represents the minimum amount of objectionable material. The system is represented in graphical form by a thermometer. The number, or the temperature of the thermometer, informs the customer about the specific content of the package as is demonstrated below in the RSAC advisories for violence:

RSAC Advisories on Violence

    0: Harmless conflict; some damage to objects
    1: Creatures injured or killed; damage to objects; fighting
    2: Humans injured or killed with small amount of blood
    3: Humans injured or killed; blood and gore
    4: Wanton and gratuitous violence, torture, and/or rape

The RSAC system does not say for whom the content is appropriate, it merely describes the content with respect to characteristics that may be of concern to parents. Since content providers fill out the questionnaire, it is a self-labeling and voluntary system. To ensure public confidence in the RSAC system, the content producer is contractually obligated to rate the content accurately and fairly. Every month a number of registered titles are randomly sampled. Producers who have willfully misrepresented the nature of their content may be fined up to $10,000 and may be required to recall their product from the shelves. Using this system, RSAC has rated over 350 game titles with 94 companies including the popular "Myst" by Broderbund, "Doom II" by id Software, and "Dark Forces" by LucasArts. Only two companies have ever requested an appeal, and so far no suits have been filed for misrepresentation.

RSACi AND PICS

During the year leading up to the passage of the Communications Decency Act at the end of 1995, a number of Internet specific labeling activities occurred: 1) the U.S. Senate Judiciary Committee heard testimony regarding the "Protection of Children From Computer Pornography Act of 1995" (S. 892); 2) the Information Highway Parental Empowerment Group (IHPEG), a coalition of three companies (Microsoft Corporation, Netscape Communications, and Progressive Networks), was formed to develop standards for empowering parents to screen inappropriate network content; 3) a number of standards for content labeling were proposed including Borenstein's and New's Internet Draft "KidCode" (June 1995); and 4) a number of services and products for blocking inappropriate content were announced, including Cyber Patrol, CyberSitter, Internet Filter, NetNanny, SurfWatch, and WebTrack.

By August, much of the standards activity was consolidated under the auspices of the World Wide Web Consortium (W3C) when the W3C, IHPEG, and twenty other organizations agreed to merge their efforts and resources to develop a standard for content selection. The result of the agreement is the Platform for Internet Content Selection (PICS) standard that allows organizations to easily define content rating systems and enable users to selectively block (or seek) information. It is important to stress that the standard is not a rating system, but an encoding method for carrying the ratings of those systems. Those encoded ratings can then be distributed with documents or through third party label bureaus.

To aid the rating of large sites, labels may apply to whole directory structures (hierarchies) of a web site if the label is appropriate to all the content. Labels can also be put on individual web pages or individual assets on a web page. This flexibility to rate at different levels is referred to as the granularity of a particular rating. The following example demonstrates a label for an RSAC label of language (l=3), sex (s=2), nudity (n=2) and violence (v=0):

(PICS-1.0 "http://www.rsac.org/v1.0/" labels

on "1994.11.05T08:15-0500" until "1995.12.31T23:59-0000"

for "http://www.gcf.org/stuff.html"

by "John Doe" ratings (l 3 s 2 n 2 v 0))

The PICS encoding specifies the rating service, version number, the creation and expiration date, the page, the rater, and the ratings themselves (other options may be specified but are not shown). Multiple labels can exist for any page. Labels can be included in html documents within the meta-tag, they can be fetched from the http server using the http get command, or they can be fetched from label bureaus. Hence, the author of a homepage could include a variety of labels on the page itself (ie, the RSAC system). The http server on which the page resides could have a label or labels for that particular page, and a third party label bureau like the "Good Housekeeping Seal of the Web" could be queried for its opinion of the quality of the web page.

The multiple distribution methods lead the authors of PICS to stress the difference between rating *systems* and rating *services*. A rating service provides content labels for information on the Internet. A rating service uses a rating system to describe the content. For instance, the Unitarian rating service and Christian Coalition rating service could both use the Motion Picture Association of America rating system to describe what each thought was the appropriate age for viewing the information.

In the rapidly evolving market of the Internet, label systems and services have a significant stake in maintaining the public confidence in the authenticity of their ratings. Malicious users who falsely label content could damage the reputation of a service, a rating system, or PICS in general. To prevent the manipulation of labels or the content to which they apply, PICS includes the capability to ensure the integrity of a label using message integrity checks (MICS) and its authenticity using digital signatures. In this way, compliant browsers can ensure that a document has not changed or been manipulated since the labeling of the document and that the label is genuine. An important part of PICS compliance is the requirement that PICS compatible clients read any label system definition from a user accessible configuration file.

In April 1996, the RSAC rating system was adapted for Internet content under the name RSACi using the PICS encoding standard. The RSACi system is a web-based questionnaire that queries the user about the content of a web page or directory tree based upon the content categories shown in Figure 1.

FIGURE 1: RSACi CONTENT ADVISORY CATEGORIES

Level 0	Level 1	Level 2	Level 3	Level 4
VIOLENCE: content may include				
Harmless conflict: some damage to objects	Creatures injured or killed; damage to objects; fighting	Humans injured or killed with small amount of blood	Humans injured or killed; blood and gore	Wanton and gratuitous violence; torture; rape
NUDITY: content may include				
No nudity or revealing attire	Revealing attire	Partial nudity	Non-sexual frontal nudity	Provocative frontal nudity
SEX: content may include				
Romance; no sex	Passionate kissing	Clothed sexual touching	Non-explicit sexual activity	Explicit sexual activity; sex crimes
LANGUAGE: content may include				
Inoffensive slang; no profanity	Mild expletives	Expletives; non-sexual anatomical references	Strong, vulgar, or hate language; obscene gestures	Crude, explicit sexual references; extreme hate language

Upon completion of the questionnaire, a PICS meta-tag similar to the one shown previously is returned to the user to be placed in the file header. There is also the option to place the RSACi symbol on the web page. The service does not currently provide message integrity checks or digital signatures. This service is currently free to anyone interested in labeling the contents of a web site. It is expected that many of the attributes of the previous RSAC system will be extended to RSACi, including the sampling of sites for labeling veracity and compliance with the terms of service that a user agrees to before receiving the label. . . .

SOME CONCERNS ABOUT RATINGS

Instability: The process of content screening and selection will continue to be highly unstable for the near future. One must remember that it is only recently that many of these standards and services became available to users of the Internet. As an example of the tremendous pace of events, consider the case of Compu-Serve. CompuServe has offered SurfWatch as part of its Internet in a Box, a suite of Internet access applications including software from Spry. A competitor of Spry, SpyGlass, has now bought SurfWatch!

Digital Signatures, Intellectual Property and Market Brand: . . . To engender public trust in labeling systems, any organization like RSAC must ensure that its labels correspond to the content, and that no unauthorized content developers use their labels and their respective icons. On the Internet, while trademarked graphical image file structures (GIFS) may be of some advantage in creating brand recognition, the important "content" with respect to selection software will be the validity of the rating that is accessed by the content seeker. How easily can this text be misappropriated? If a digital signature is provided by RSAC and checked by the browsers for authenticity, it is very difficult. If digital signatures are not incorporated, it can be misused very easily. One could create such a label for an adult web service without consulting the RSAC questionnaire, and one may do so with malicious intent. Hence, simple encryption technologies would seem to provide the only protection to widely-used labeling systems.

International Issues: The threat of governmental censorship of electronic media provided the main impetus for the formation of RSAC and the development of PICS. Until this point, we have only considered this issue with respect to the United States. However, an oft cited characteristic of the digital realm is its global scope. This can increase the difficulty of developing a content labeling system because the cultural norms of violence, language, sexuality, and political freedoms differ across the globe, and there are no cultural boundaries in cyberspace. Hence, content which may be considered appropriate within one culture may be considered inappropriate to others. Governments have been attempting to legislate technical infrastructure requirements because of indecency or cultural concerns.

An immediate difficulty with evaluative labeling systems is that what may be appropriate for one culture may be highly inappropriate for another. Fortunately, the PICS system allows for multiple rating systems, services, and label bureaus. As an example of a potential problem, consider the aversion for Nazi propaganda by the German government. Without requiring draconian regulation of infrastructure or Internet Service Providers (ISPs),

Germany could require that all browsers and ISPs use a labeling system and label bureau for filtering information pertaining to Nazism. All PICS compliant browsers must be able to read label system definitions from a configuration file, and the government could be responsible for developing the appropriate rating and labeling services. However, this technique can also be extended even further by totalitarian nations such as China to filter sensitive information, if all access is required to go through gateways that employ filtering software.

Regardless, RSACi has an advantage in the international market because systems that use straightforward content description rather than age appropriate evaluations will have greater applicability and adaptability across multiple cultures. While there is some cultural bias within the RSAC system, efforts to extend the system while keeping it very content oriented would allow it to have international scope. Some countries may associate different icons or names with the ratings differently, but the numeric value of a descriptive rating would stay the same. Potentially, this would extend usage of the RSACi system beyond the United States to become an international content labeling service.

A common saying among those that study the Internet is that, "three months are one Web year." However, there are a number of observations one can make about content labeling today. One observation is that this market is extraordinarily dynamic. Many of the filtering companies discussed in this case study are one to three years old. Some of the companies will likely go out of business, or be purchased or bought by larger content or infrastructure organizations—as has happened with SurfWatch.

The dynamic nature of the Internet leads one to realize the importance of balancing healthy competition with cooperation on sensitive social issues between the entities discussed. With the chaotic development and flow of information on the Internet, it is also important that standards such as PICS are being adopted at each level of information delivery to bring some sense of order and control to concerned users. It is in this spirit of cooperation that disparate organizations such as RSAC and Microsoft have worked together to use the PICS encoding system to develop a content labeling and blocking mechanism and to make the system available as widely as possible. The ultimate goal of such content advisory systems is to provide a technical alternative to government regulation and censorship of the Internet and to empower members of the public to make informed decisions based upon their own value systems about the appropriateness of content when accessing the web.

VIEWPOINT

6

"While self-rating may sound
innocuous, it would likely have the
effect of banishing controversial
expression to the outer margins of
cyberspace."

SELF-RATING OF INTERNET SITES
WILL VIOLATE FREE SPEECH

Nadine Strossen

Nadine Strossen is the president of the American Civil Liberties
Union (ACLU), an organization that works to defend Americans'
civil rights. She is also a professor at New York Law School. In
the following viewpoint, Strossen opposes systems in which
website producers rate the sexual and violent content of their
products. She maintains that such systems will undermine free
expression by coercing Internet providers to limit or discourage
controversial speech. Sites that offer advice on topics such as
AIDS may find themselves at the mercy of the "Internet gatekeepers," she contends. Strossen supports efforts to provide descriptive information on Internet sites most appropriate for children instead of limiting everyone's access to Internet sites.

As you read, consider the following questions:
1. According to Strossen, in what way are Internet self-rating
   systems similar to regulations in the music, video, and movie
   industries?
2. How does the experience of Kiyoshi Kuromiya illustrate the
   threat of on-line self-rating, in the author's opinion?
3. What "lifeless medium" will the Internet resemble if self-
   rating systems are imposed, according to Strossen?

Reprinted from Nadine Strossen, "Burning Down the Net," ACLU white paper, October
2, 1997, by permission of the American Civil Liberties Union.

Despite the Supreme Court's landmark decision in *Reno v. ACLU*, striking down the Communications Decency Act (CDA), online free speech continues to be embattled.

Less than a month after our Supreme Court victory in June 1997, the White House called an "Internet Summit" with industry leaders and the "pro-family" organizations that had joined the administration in championing the CDA, to pursue an industry-wide system for rating and blocking online expression. But such government-pressured industry "self-regulation" could well suppress the same controversial speech and non-mainstream speakers that the CDA would have targeted more directly.

VOLUNTARY COERCION

Sound familiar? In 1996, the White House called a meeting with television industry leaders, pressing them to devise a "voluntary" ratings scheme for the V-chip. As we have since seen, political protests about the industry's proposed scheme forced it to formulate another, more draconian plan. Further belying the allegedly "voluntary" nature of this ratings system is the Federal Communications Commission's veto power over it.

Thus, the TV ratings follow in a long line of purported "self-regulatory" measures that in fact are coerced by threats of more direct government control. We previously saw the same pattern, for example, in the music, video and movie industries. And all such schemes have had the same suppressive impact: stifling the diversity and accessibility of expression in the affected media.

We must not let the Internet—which the Supreme Court hailed as "the most participatory form of mass speech yet developed"—suffer the same fate.

Since learning about the schemes to regulate controversial cyberspeech that were touted at the White House summit, I have been alarmed at computer industry leaders' eagerness to join CDA advocates in jumping on the blocking bandwagon. To be sure, no single proposal will necessarily constrict cybercommunications. Nonetheless, I am troubled by the rush to embrace self-regulatory regimes, and the failure to examine the longer-term dangers that they pose to our precious freedoms. Certainly, the history of similar ventures in other communications industries should at least give us pause.

PRO-DECENCY OR ANTI-FREEDOM?

Precisely to inject such a cautionary note into the discussion, in September 1997 the ACLU issued a white paper entitled "Fahrenheit 451.2: Is Cyberspace Burning? How Rating and Blocking

Proposals May Torch Free Speech on the Internet." As this report explains, even considered separately, each proposed "voluntary" regulation poses smoldering threats to online free speech; when considered as a whole, they set off the smoke detectors.

While self-rating may sound innocuous, it would likely have the effect of banishing controversial expression to the outer margins of cyberspace, where it is for all practical purposes inaccessible to many would-be readers.

Policing the Internet

MUSIC IS A BOND. MY KITTY AND I LOVE THE SAX.

SEX WITH YOUR CAT? SICK, SICK, SICK! I'M REPORTING YOU TO THE CENSORS!

Consider the impact of online self-rating upon one of our clients in *Reno v. ACLU*, Kiyoshi Kuromiya. He operates Critical Path AIDS Project, a web site that offers safer sex information in street language with explicit diagrams, designed to reach teenagers. Kuromiya doesn't want to apply a stigmatizing rating such as "explicit" to his site, since that would cause it to be blocked. But under current proposals, unrated sites will also be blocked. So either way, his site will end up being blocked. Moreover, if he gave it a rating with which some "pro-decency" organization or politician disagreed, he could well face penalties.

Senator Patty Murray (D-WA), from the home state of industry titan Microsoft, has already proposed a law that imposes criminal penalties for "misratings." And a major filtering software company, Safe Surf, has proposed another federal law that would authorize parents to sue online speakers for damages resulting from "negligent misratings" of their speech. Not coincidentally, such industry leaders have an economic stake in schemes that would solidify their role as Internet gatekeepers. And the gate may well slam shut on non-commercial, less powerful, and more controversial entities and individuals, such as Kuromiya.

PREVENTING FREE SPEECH FIRES

In evaluating purportedly voluntary schemes for regulating the Internet, we should always keep in mind the Supreme Court's core conclusion in *Reno v. ACLU*: that the Net is analogous to the print media, and hence entitled to the maximum First Amendment protection. Drawing on that analogy, we should pursue in the cyber context the types of measures that help readers and parents make informed decisions about the books and other print publications to choose for themselves or their children.

For example, we applaud the American Library Association's "Guide to Cyberspace for Parents and Kids," which lists some of "the most educational and entertaining" sites for children.

We also urge the software industry to develop products that maximize user information and control. Contrary to their current practice, producers of blocking software should inform customers which sites they block. Additionally, users should be able to adjust the products to reflect their own values, and to take into account the particular maturity levels of their own children.

While sounding the fire alarm about these new threats to Internet free speech, the ACLU's white paper ends on a positive note, calling on other cyber-libertarians to join us in stamping out the cinders before they become an Internet inferno: "It is not too late for the Internet community to . . . carefully examine these proposals and to reject those that will transform the Internet from a true marketplace of ideas into just another mainstream, lifeless medium with content no more exciting or diverse than that of television."

The title of the ACLU's paper poses the crucial question: "Is Cyberspace Burning?" In answering that question for you, . . . I'd like to paraphrase Smokey the Bear: "Only you can prevent free speech fires."

PERIODICAL BIBLIOGRAPHY

The following articles have been selected to supplement the diverse views presented in this chapter. Addresses are provided for periodicals not indexed in the *Readers' Guide to Periodical Literature*, the *Alternative Press Index*, the *Social Sciences Index*, or the *Index to Legal Periodicals and Books*.

Michael A. Banks	"Filtering the Net in Libraries: The Case (Mostly) in Favor," *Computers in Libraries*, March 1998. Available from 143 Old Marlton Pike, Medford, NJ 08055-8750.
David Brake	"Surfing with the Blinkers On," *New Scientist*, April 6, 1996. Available from King's Reach Tower, Stamford St., SE1 9LS, London, England.
Dan Carney	"Court Strikes Down Ban on Internet 'Indecency,'" *Congressional Quarterly Weekly Report*, June 28, 1997.
David Coursey	"Where Everybody Knows Your Name," *Computerworld*, February 10, 1997. Available from 551 Old Connecticut Path, Box 9171, Framingham, MA 01701-9171.
Economist	"Hands Off the Internet," July 5, 1997.
Pam Greenberg	"The Omnipresent Internet," *State Legislatures*, April 1997. Available from 1560 Broadway, Suite 700, Denver, CO 80202-5140.
Mark Hanson	"Supreme Spree: Court Decides on Everything from Federalism to the Internet," *ABA Journal*, August 1997.
Mike High	"Decency and Indecency in Cyberspace," *Poets and Writers Magazine*, July/August 1997. Available from 72 Spring St., New York, NY 10012.
Kenneth Jost	"Children's Television: Will the New Regulations Make It Better?" *CQ Researcher*, August 15, 1997. Available from 1414 22nd St. NW, Washington, DC 20037.
Kathryn Munro	"Monitor a Child's Access," *PC Magazine*, March 24, 1998. Available from 1 Park Ave., New York, NY 10016.
New York Times	"More Join Challenge to Library over Blocking of Internet Sites," February 9, 1998.

James Podgers   "Internet Regulations, Round Three; Reno Was
                         Only One Step in Determining Government's
                         Role, Panelists Say," *ABA Journal*, March 1998.

Robert J. Posch Jr.   "Another Win for Internet Self-Regulation,"
                         Direct Marketing, September 1997. Available
                         from 224 Seventh St., Garden City, NY 11530.

Joshua Quittner   "@ the Supreme Court: Some Surprisingly
                         Wired Justices Hear an Antiporn Case That
                         Would Restrict Free Speech in Cyberspace,"
                         Time, March 31, 1997.

Michael Rogers   "Internet Blocking Software: Online Savior or
                         Scourge?" *Library Journal*, April 1, 1997.
                         Available from 249 W. 17th St., New York, NY
                         10011.

Ira Teinowitz   "Internet Privacy Concerns Addressed,"
                         Advertising Age, June 16, 1997. Available from
                         740 Rush St., Chicago, IL 60611.

CHAPTER 5

ARE TELEVISION CONTENT REGULATIONS BENEFICIAL FOR CHILDREN?

CHAPTER PREFACE

When Congress passed the Telecommunications Act of 1996, it did more than lift restrictions on the telephone and cable industries. The law also included a provision requiring manufacturers to install a V-chip—a device that allows parents to block inappropriate programming from their televisions—in all television sets larger than 13 inches. The V-chip has received considerable support from Congress and even from the television industry. As stated by Madeline Levine, the author of *Viewing Violence: How Media Violence Affects Your Child's and Adolescent's Development*, the V-chip returns "some measure of control to parents who feel both horrified and helpless by the onslaught of fictional violence that their children face."

However, the V-chip is criticized for various reasons. Some people believe that the V-chip will undermine parents' responsibility for monitoring their children's viewing habits. Dan Andriacco, the director of the Communications Office of the Roman Catholic Archdiocese of Cincinnati, argues that parents, not technology, should exercise ultimate control over the types of television shows their children watch. "Parents are the ultimate V-chips because they can draw distinctions guided by love, values, and sense," he maintains. Andriacco worries that parents will become increasingly complacent if they believe that the V-chip is doing their work for them.

Even supporters of television regulation have attacked the use of the V-chip because it depends on a rating system developed by the entertainment industry. Many people believe that the industry cannot be trusted to rate itself. Some critics of the V-chip are also concerned that use of the device will free television producers from the responsibility to air appropriate programming because they might assume that the V-chip has done the censoring for them. With the advent of the V-chip, opponents argue, future television producers may feel free to edit content even less than they do currently. As a result, these critics contend, television may become more violent and sexually explicit.

While the V-chip promises to offer some relief to parents who are struggling to limit their children's exposure to violent and sexually explicit television programming, many argue that it should not be regarded as a cure-all. The V-chip and other measures to regulate the content of children's television are debated in the following chapter.

| "The V-chip is not a substitute for parents. It is a tool for parents."

THE V-CHIP WILL PROTECT CHILDREN FROM TELEVISION VIOLENCE

Gloria Tristani

The V-chip is a computer device placed in television sets that allows parents to block violent content. In 1996, Congress passed legislation requiring the installation of V-chips in new television sets. In the following viewpoint, Gloria Tristani, commissioner of the Federal Communications Commission, supports the legislation. She describes what she believes to be excessive violence on television and claims that the V-chip is a useful tool that enables parents to monitor their children's viewing habits.

As you read, consider the following questions:
1. According to Tristani, what are the effects of children's exposure to television violence?
2. Why do today's parents need the help that the V-chip provides, according to the author?
3. How has the television industry revised its rating system to accommodate the V-chip, according to the author?

Excerpted from Gloria Tristani, "Children and TV Violence," speech delivered to the Puerto Rican Congress on Television Violence, San Juan, PR, February 11, 1998.

I am pleased to address the issue of children and violence in the media. Children are our most precious resource, but all too often their voices aren't heard when public issues are discussed. It may be because children have no vote, no Washington lobbyists, no money to donate to their favorite candidate. It is up to us, each of us, to speak for them, to protect them and to honor them. So, on behalf of the children of this great country, I am pleased to be here today.

I would like to address two questions this morning. First, how does TV, and especially violence on TV, affect our children? Second, what can we do about it?

There isn't much doubt that TV has an impact on children. 98% of American homes own a TV set—more than the percentage of homes that own a telephone. The average child watches about 25 hours of television a week—more time each year watching TV than he or she spends in the classroom.

And, much of what kids are watching on TV is violent. By the time they complete elementary school, children in the United States have witnessed about 8,000 murders and 100,000 acts of violence. And while prime-time TV contains about 5 violent acts per hour—bad enough—there are over 20 violent acts per hour on children's programming. Each week, television programming contains about 800 violent scenes that qualify as high risk for younger children.

THE DEBATE IS OVER

So children watch a lot of TV, and a lot of what they watch is violent. Is this a serious problem? Absolutely. Over 1,000 studies indicate that there is a link between TV violence and children's aggressive attitudes and anti-social behavior. These studies were conducted by groups like the American Medical Association, the National Academy of Sciences, the United States Surgeon General and the National Institute of Mental Health. As one researcher put it: "The scientific debate is over." Television violence teaches aggressive and anti-social behavior to children.

In addition, there are other, less obvious, impacts of TV violence on children. Studies have found that exposure to TV violence is linked to an increase in criminal activity, increased desensitization to violence and an increase in indifference to victims. Violence on television can also make children more afraid of the world. One study reported that violence on TV can cause children to show "an exaggerated fear of being attacked by a violent assailant." One researcher refers to this as the "mean and scary world syndrome." Finally, TV violence affects different children differently. Very young children, for instance, have a hard time connecting punishment which may occur later in a program with violence that occurred earlier. Thus, violent acts must be punished and must be punished quickly if a young child is to learn that violence is punished and not rewarded.

Whose responsibility is it to protect children from television violence?

First and most clearly, it is the obligation of the parents to protect their children from television programming that they believe is inappropriate. Research indicates that when parents take an active role in the selection of television programs, children select different programs to watch.

Second, it is the obligation of the entertainment industry to acknowledge the importance of reducing the level of violence on programs that children are watching. The industry could take a huge step forward by acknowledging this responsibility and finding ways to reduce the amount of harmful violent images on these programs.

Third, it is the responsibility of society. It is up to each of us to convey the message to the entertainment industry, to our children, and to each other that harmful violence in programs that children watch will not be tolerated. We would not knowingly let someone into our homes who could harm our children. Then why, as a society, should we allow our children to be exposed to harmful violence on TV? Parents need the tools to protect their children.

No Substitute for Parents

There are some steps that the government can take. We can give parents the tools to protect their children from material that they believe is inappropriate. That's the V-chip. . . .

First, the V-chip. As many of you know, Congress enacted V-chip legislation as part of the 1996 Telecommunications Act. For those of you who may not be familiar with the V-chip law, let me briefly explain how it works and then give you a status report.

The V-chip is not a substitute for parents. It is a tool for parents. Parents cannot always monitor what their children watch on TV. Nowadays there aren't just three channels to monitor, there are dozens. No parent can possibly know what's on all of them all of the time. And in this age of single parent families and families in which both parents must work to make ends meet, it isn't possible for parents to always be at home to monitor their children's television viewing. The V-chip will allow parents to block violent, sexual or other programming that they believe is harmful to their children. When the parents leave for work, or go out for the evening and leave the children with a babysitter, they will be able to punch a couple of buttons and the V-chip will block out programming that they do not wish their children to see.

How will the V-chip permit parents to block shows? Well, along with requiring V-chip blocking technology in new sets, Congress also required that program ratings be developed, so that the V-chip would be able to tell what kind of programming was being shown. The ratings will be sent by the TV station or cable operator over what's called the "vertical blanking interval." I'm sure all of you know the horizontal line on your sets that sometimes needs to be adjusted. That's not just there to annoy you. That line can carry a lot of valuable information, like closed captioning for the hearing impaired. It will also carry the TV ratings system when it's ultimately in place. The V-chip will be able to read those signals and will block the show if it has been programmed to do so.

PROTECTING CHILDREN FROM OFFENSIVE SPEECH

I believe that this kind of tool is fully consistent with the First Amendment. By using the V-chip, parents can protect their children from offensive speech. As former FCC Chairman Newton Minow said, if the V-chip is unconstitutional, so is a remote-control device—and so, too, are parents who control what their children watch by turning off the television or limiting television viewing time. I'm a strong believer in free speech. But I'm also a strong believer in the health and well-being of our children. I do not believe that these goals are mutually exclusive.

Congress gave the TV industry the first chance to develop a voluntary ratings system and directed the FCC to determine whether the industry's voluntary system satisfied the goals of the statute. If the industry system was found unacceptable, then the FCC was to establish an advisory committee and come up with a ratings system of its own.

Now, as many of you know, in 1997 the industry (the National Association of Broadcasters, the National Cable Television Association and the Motion Picture Association of America) submitted a voluntary ratings system for FCC approval. In many ways, the system was similar to the movies ratings system— from "TV-G" for general audiences to "TV-MA" for mature audiences only. Programming specifically designed for children had its own ratings—"TV-Y" for programs suitable for all children and "TV-Y7" for programs designed for children 7 and above.

The industry proposed that the ratings would be applied to all programs except news, sports and unedited movies on premium cable channels. The rating would generally be applied by a program's producer or distributor, although a local station would retain the right to substitute a rating it deemed appropriate for its particular community. The industry began displaying its ratings as small icons in the upper left-hand corner of the screen for the first 15 seconds of each show—perhaps you've seen them. The industry also established an Oversight Monitoring Board to ensure that the ratings were applied accurately and consistently.

A Tool for Parents

The V-Chip is a tool that a parent can use to help monitor a child's television viewing. Parents will still have the responsibility. Parents will need to become more aware of what types of programs are suitable for particular ages of children. Until now, television programs were aimed at a general audience. The problem is a program suitable for a "general audience" is often not suitable for a five-year-old.

Mary Ann Bunta, National Coalition on Television Violence Website, October 19, 1997.

After the industry submitted its proposal, the Commission received literally thousands of comments, letters and e-mails from different groups and individuals, like the PTA, the American Medical Association and the Children's Defense Fund. Most of the comments we received objected to the industry's proposed ratings system. They generally argued that parents needed more information than the industry system provided. They argued that parents not only want to know that a program may not be suitable for kids under 14 because it *may* contain violence, sex or coarse language, but that parents want to know which of those the show *actually does* contain. In other words, they argued that parents want to know the *content* of the program that led to the rating.

After discussions with family and child advocacy groups, the industry agreed to revise its ratings system. To their existing ratings system industry added content indicators—"S" for sex, "V" for violence, "L" for language and "D" for suggestive dialogue. So now, for example, a show could be rated TV-PG-V, which means that it was rated PG because of its violent content. The industry also added a content label to kids' programming—"FV" for fantasy violence. The industry also agreed to add five members of the advocacy community to the Oversight Monitoring Board. . . .

A Challenge to Parents and the Entertainment Industry

I challenge parents to take an interest in the programs their children are watching and talk about the content of the programs and commercials with their children. Parents should also contact their local stations. Let them know what you like and don't like about their programming.

I also challenge those in the entertainment industry—substantially reduce the violent content in programs that children watch and voluntarily include in violent programming the very real consequences of violent acts and punishment for the perpetrator.

Finally, I challenge each of us to speak out publicly and say that violence in programs that children watch will no longer be tolerated. I also urge you to watch more TV with your children. Find and support the good programs. [Former CBS president] Fred Friendly once said that broadcasters make so much money doing their worst that they cannot afford to do their best. I hope that someday we can prove him wrong.

"The long-term effect of the
requirement to rate television
programming will be to make shows
more violent and explicit."

THE V-CHIP WILL NOT PROTECT CHILDREN FROM TELEVISION VIOLENCE

Bob Gale

In 1996, Congress passed legislation requiring that all new televisions be equipped with a computer chip that allows violent programs to be blocked. In the following viewpoint, Bob Gale argues that the V-chip will actually increase violence on television because broadcasters will assume that parents are using the chip to monitor their child's viewing, relieving the broadcasters of the responsibility to air shows that are appropriate for children. In addition, he claims that the "R" rating used for movies encourages filmmakers to include excessive foul language and violence because the rating is the same whether language and violence occur once or repeatedly. The "V" rating on television shows will have a similar effect, Gale concludes. Gale wrote and coproduced the three *Back to the Future* films.

As you read, consider the following questions:
1. Why does the author believe that the "V" rating for television shows will have no more effect than the "R" rating for movies?
2. According to Gale, what was the result of the 1954 congressional hearings about comic books?
3. What does the author believe is the true cause of juvenile delinquency?

Reprinted from Bob Gale, "Fans of Sex and Violence Will Love the V-Chip," *The Wall Street Journal*, February 21, 1996, by permission of the Center for the Study of Popular Culture, Los Angeles.

N otice to all politicians, interest groups and citizens who are endorsing the V-chip as a way to reduce sex and violence on TV: The long-term effect of the requirement to rate television programming will be to make shows more violent and explicit.

Theoretically, a program rated for objectionable content would be blocked from view on a V-chip-equipped TV set unless overridden by the viewer. Let's look at movies to see what happens to content under a rating system.

THE R RATING

An "R" rating is given to a movie with a certain level of sex, violence and/or profanity, and is supposed to prohibit children under 17 from seeing the film without an accompanying adult. If the "F" word is used in a movie, it guarantees an R rating, whether the expletive is used once, twice, or a hundred times. If a producer has decided the film is going to get an R rating, there is no reason to be concerned about the language. The same applies, up to a certain point, for sexual or violent content. If you decide to show somebody's brains getting blown out, why stop at one? Why not three or four or 20?

The R rating is society's way of saying that it's OK to have violent/sexual/profane movies as long as they are labeled as such. Mom and dad can take the kids to see it; it's their responsibility, and they have been warned.

I don't have a problem with R-rated movies; I've made some myself. But I've been to R-rated movies where 10-year-olds are looking at blood and guts and sex and hearing some pretty rough language. Why did the parents bring the kid? Probably because they wanted to see the movie, and couldn't get a baby-sitter, or realized that a child's admission ticket is cheaper than a baby-sitter.

THE V RATING

How does this experience apply to the V-chip for TV? Let's assume that a violent show will get a "V" rating. At the beginning maybe there will be some sort of stigma attached to a show rated V. Maybe some advertisers will shun these shows. But that'll last only until someone comes out with a V-rated show that gets huge ratings. Once an audience develops for these shows, the V rating will have no more stigma than an "R" does at the movies. So the TV producer who is making "Chainsaw Squad" is going to say to himself, "I know my show is going to be rated V; it's inevitable. Since my audience accepts violence, I'm going to increase the body count, and be even more graphic with it." The V rating makes violence acceptable. Once the concept of violence becomes acceptable, it's just a matter of how much.

But let's go even further. The network executive is going to say, "Gee, in the old days we'd have put this show on at 10 p.m.—we'd have been considered irresponsible if we had put it on at an hour when kids were awake. But since the V-chip will prevent kids from seeing it without adult supervision, we're going to put 'Chainsaw Squad' on at 8 p.m." So then dad wants to watch "Chainsaw Squad," and the kid, who's awake anyway, watches it too. Is dad going to turn the channel? Probably not. And don't forget about the teenage brother. He knows how to defeat the V-chip, no doubt for the same reason he can use a computer and his parents can't.

AN ABDICATION OF PARENTAL RESPONSIBILITY

Although using the v-chip would perhaps salve the conscience of parents who rely on TV as an electronic baby-sitter, it would really be an abdication of parental responsibility. Cartoonist Jim Borgmann showed this when he depicted two fourth-graders sitting in front of a television, one saying: "Looks like the v-chip is blocking this show . . . Let's go catch a smoke." Pointedly, the kids are alone. Their parents may feel safe being absent because the v-chip is present. The whole job of the device is to take over the parents' role in protecting children from harmful TV violence.

Dan Andriacco, *U.S. Catholic*, June 1996.

"But parents will never be that irresponsible," you say. No? My daughter is seven. I'm very strict about what movies she can see. But other kids in her class see PG-13 movies. Then I hear the parents complain about the content. So I say, "But the movie was rated PG-13. That means you shouldn't take a seven-year-old." And they say, "Yeah, but I don't go by that," or "But the commercials made it look okay," or "Yeah, but they're promoting it at McDonald's." The warning applies to everyone else, but not to them.

BREAKDOWN OF THE FAMILY

In 1954, there were congressional hearings about comic books. A child psychiatrist named Frederic Wertham wrote a book in which he claimed that comic books were a leading cause of juvenile delinquency. As a result of these hearings comic books were sanitized, but delinquency rates didn't change at all. Guess what? The real cause of juvenile delinquency wasn't comic books! And it's not television or movies or music. The cause then was the same as it is today: the breakdown of the family.

The V-chip will not make parents more intelligent or more responsible. The V-chip won't prevent teenage pregnancy. It won't encourage two-parent households or strengthen family life. We in the media can make shows in which we say that crime doesn't pay, but as long as crime does pay, people will commit crimes. We can make shows that tell viewers not to have babies out of wedlock, but as long as the government pays more money to unwed mothers for each additional child they bear, well, money talks.

There are lots of serious social problems in America. The V-chip won't solve any of them—and it certainly will not improve broadcast content.

"After carefully weighing the alternatives, we opted for a system that is simple to use and easy to understand."

TELEVISION RATINGS WILL PROTECT CHILDREN FROM VIOLENCE

Jack Valenti

In the following viewpoint, Jack Valenti advocates a television ratings system based on age and content. Because the rating system is simple and easy to use, Valenti argues, parents will be able to make better decisions in advance about the kinds of programming their children will watch. The author believes that an age and content rating system, rather than a pure content system, will play an important role in keeping children from watching inappropriate programming. Valenti is chairman and CEO of the Motion Picture Association of America, an organization that represents the American film industry.

As you read, consider the following questions:

1. Why does the author believe that age-based ratings are better than ratings for "sex," "violence," and "language"?
2. According to the author, why did the Canadians abandon their rating system?
3. How will the new rating system help parents who leave their children in the care of a baby-sitter, according to Valenti?

Reprinted from Jack Valenti, "The Television Ratings System Is Simple and User-Friendly," *Los Angeles Times*, January 3, 1997, by permission of the author.

The entire television community has banded together—for the first time—to offer guidelines to parents so they can better monitor their young children's TV watching. The guidelines are in effect now. The U.S. is the only nation to implement a parental TV assistance plan.

Yet in spite of this extraordinary, totally voluntary effort, there have been savage attacks on the guidelines by politicians and newspaper editorials. It is odd that these harsh criticisms were issued before the guidelines were completed and publicly declared.

What are the critics complaining about? They want more information, such as "S, V, L" (for sex, violence, language) attached to each program. Further, they claim the guidelines are "not content-based." That these criticisms cannot bear the light of sober scrutiny lessens in no way the anger of the onslaughts.

RATING PROBLEMS

We gave intense thought to ratings for sex, violence and language, and concluded that they wouldn't work. An S rating would have to be applied to Dr. Quinn, Medicine Woman, which has been praised for its family values (sex in this program is mild to almost nonexistent but for accuracy the rating would have to be applied). "S" would also have to be assigned to Sharon Stone's film Basic Instinct. How would parents, unaware of the content of these shows, make a distinction between the two?

A V rating would be attached to the movie Natural Born Killers but also to National Geographic's Explorer and The Three Stooges. How are parents to sort out the violent content in those programs? How indeed.

No problem, say the critics. Merely apply intensity values, such as V-4, S-5, L-2. Fine, except for two reasons.

First, Canada experimented with this very scheme. On Dec. 18, 1996, however, the Canadians announced that they had abandoned that design and were working on a simpler plan, much nearer to the American model. Why? Canadian parents were confused by the detailed ranking system and befuddled by a remote controller that sometimes required keying in five buttons just to get the system going. Too complicated; as one wag put it, "Calculus is easier."

Second, the folks in charge of American newspapers' TV pages plainly state there isn't enough space in the daily logs grid to print lengthy descriptions. The Newspaper Assn. of America has bluntly warned us that unless our symbols were brief, no newspaper would publish them. Indeed, to make it more difficult, the very newspapers that urged more information for parents will not print more information unless it is very concise.

SIMPLE AND EASY

After carefully weighing the alternatives, we opted for a system that is simple to use and easy to understand. We mingled content and age, which works for parents. Under our system, Dr. Quinn, Medicine Woman would be put into category TV-G, meaning for the entire family. Whereas Basic Instinct (if unedited) would be put in TV-M, (meaning "mature" content) specifically for adults and not for children.

THE PROBLEM WITH CONTENT LABELS

Several consumer organizations . . . argue that age ratings fail to provide parents with sufficient information. They want content labels added to the age categories to inform parents about whether programs contain sex, violence or profane language. Under their proposal, a program might be rated, for example, "TV-14 for S, V and L."

But such a system wouldn't give parents that much more information. They would have no way of knowing whether . . . V (violence) means one punch or many. Such labeling is far too vague to be of value, and it focuses on content without regard for context, on quantifiable incidents rather than on the intent or the significance or appropriateness of the incidents.

James M. Wall, Christian Century, January 1–8, 1997.

If parents go to dinner at 7:30 p.m. and leave their 6-year-old and 8-year-old in the charge of a 16-year-old baby sitter, they are not going to be able to sit in front of their TV set and see the beginning of every program. What to do if they don't know the content of programs because newspapers are not printing in advance lengthy descriptions? Under TV parental guidelines, they can make decisions quickly, in advance. They punch two buttons and block out TV-14 and TV-M or to play it safe for the very young, also block out TV-PG. They can now go to dinner knowing they have made choices easily, quickly and carefully.

Respected journalist Steven Roberts summed it up neatly: "This [rating system] is too commonsensical for the self-appointed guardians of children. We suspect that after years of trying to get the broadcasters to pay attention to them, they can't take yes for an answer."

"It's clear that the nation's parents need more protection from fatuous reformers than their kids do from Baywatch."

TELEVISION RATINGS WILL NOT PROTECT CHILDREN FROM VIOLENCE

Frank Rich

In the following viewpoint, Frank Rich, a columnist for the *New York Times*, argues that the debate over television ratings masks the larger problem of the coarsening of American culture. He believes that rating television programs, or installing a V-chip to make parental regulation possible, will ultimately fail to change Americans' viewing habits. The rating system will also be ineffective because it will not apply to television commercials.

As you read, consider the following questions:

1. What does the author mean when he says the debate over television ratings is an "escapist sideshow"?
2. According to the author, why will American viewing habits remain unchanged by television ratings?
3. What does Rich believe parents should do if they are concerned about their children watching coarse television programs?

Reprinted from Frank Rich, "The PG-Files," *The New York Times*, December 18, 1996, p. A19, by permission. Copyright ©1996 by The New York Times.

It's always heartwarming to watch show-business executives, professional child advocates, Congressmen and even the President fret over the television habits of America's youth. But after listening to the great and heated debate over the TV ratings that Jack Valenti will hand down with fanfare worthy of Moses and the Ten Commandments, it's clear that the nation's parents need more protection from fatuous reformers than their kids do from *Baywatch*.

The gist of the debate is as simplistic as it is beside the point. Mr. Valenti, the Hollywood lobbyist masterminding the ratings system, favors rating TV shows by age appropriateness à la the movie ratings he created 28 years ago. Everyone else wants ratings that label programming for its specific violent, sexual or four-letter content.

AN ESCAPIST SIDESHOW

What no one will say is that even if content ratings prevail—which they should and eventually will—we'll still be almost back where we started. The ratings debate is not only in itself a fount of intellectually vacuous chat-show TV—how many politicians can dance on the head of a V-chip?—but is an escapist sideshow deflecting attention from any real discussion about the coarsening of our culture and the growing stranglehold of video in all its forms (including video games and the Internet's own junk programming) over the young, who watch 1,000 hours a year of TV alone.

Parents do deserve all the information they can get in helping to guide their children's viewing habits, and if more details are added by a ratings system, that will be a plus. But only a small plus. Such ratings will solely benefit parents who are already attentive to their children's TV diet and already know much of the information these ratings will convey.

Any parent who either doesn't yet know or care that the prime-time hour starting at 8 P.M. is filled with sex-obsessed sitcoms—or that 10 P.M. shows like *N.Y.P.D. Blue* are not for children—or that pay-cable services like HBO and Showtime present unedited R-rated movies—is unlikely to heed detailed ratings now. And one need only look at those other ratings, the Nielsens, to see that these parents are in the vast majority.

A PUSH-BUTTON PANACEA

Nor will that great push-button panacea, the V-chip, rescue parents in either camp. For this Rube Goldberg invention to be effective, parents will have to replace every set in their household or equip every one with the device—a gesture that is not only costly but, again, will be carried out only by parents already on the case. Even those parents, however, may soon be in the market for family counseling. If they program their sets to block shows rated as inappropriate for 8-year-olds, they're going to have to answer to their angry teen-agers. (This is assuming that a nation incapable of programming its VCR's will bother to activate the V-chip, once proudly installed, in the first place.)

CHANGING VIEWERS' HABITS

Just as ratings and the V-chip are unlikely to change American TV habits (any more than movie ratings have elevated moviegoing habits), so the debate about them has been a sea of red herrings. Much noise has been made about the fact that it's a "conflict of interest" for Hollywood to rate its own products, for instance, but what exactly is the alternative? Who will pay for and choose the ideological complexion of a huge bureaucracy that will have to be on 24-hour call to rate 2,000 hours of programming per day? No one has raised the more important issue of why commercials won't be rated—some are sexier than *Friends*, and sugary cereals can do more damage to kids than most TV—or why violent sports also get a free pass.

Reprinted by permission of Ed Gamble.

But these forgotten questions, too, pale against the big one of our national addiction to junk and our refusal to take any personal responsibility for that behavior. It's adult consumers with spending power who drive the TV marketplace and set the example for the young; if adults were serious about eliminating coarse TV, they would turn off *Married . . . With Children* and refuse to subscribe to risqué cable channels. Sponsors would flee, cancellations would follow, channels would die. American children will never grow up in a healthier electronic environment unless their parents grow up first.

| "We need a safety net for the bad broadcasters."

REQUIRING MORE HOURS OF EDUCATIONAL TELEVISION WILL BENEFIT CHILDREN

Gigi B. Sohn

In July 1996, the Federal Communications Commission (FCC) and television broadcasters agreed to a policy that requires broadcasters to air three hours of children's educational programs per week. In the following viewpoint, which was written before the agreement was finalized, Gigi B. Sohn supports the plan. She maintains that because broadcasters have free use of the airwaves, they are required to serve the needs of the public—including children's need for quality programming. Children should not be required to depend on public broadcasting for their educational needs, she insists, nor should they be forced to depend only on programming aired before 7 A.M. Without such a required safety net, she believes, broadcasters will have little incentive to look after the educational needs of children. Sohn is deputy director of the Media Access Project, a Washington, D.C., public interest law firm that promotes the public's right to media access.

As you read, consider the following questions:

1. Why is broadcaster opposition to the required three hours of educational television "audacious," in Sohn's opinion?
2. How does the author respond to the criticism that educational and informational programming cannot be defined?
3. According to Sohn, why is it insufficient to rely on cable for educational programming?

Reprinted from Gigi B. Sohn, "Safety Net Necessary for Bad Broadcasters," *San Diego North County Times*, July 14, 1996. Reprinted by permission of Scripps-Howard News Service and United Media.

It is amazing, yet all too predictable, that television broadcast-ers are fighting a Federal Communications Commission (FCC) proposal that would require them to show a mere three hours of children's educational and informational programming each week.

Broadcasters get free use of the valuable public airwaves, and in exchange they are required, as trustees of those airwaves, to serve the needs of their communities.

A DIET OF VIOLENCE

Children are perhaps the segment of the population most in need of good broadcast programming. In the absence of solid educational fare on commercial television, kids will be left with a diet of violence and toy-driven programming.

What makes broadcasters' opposition to the FCC's proposal so audacious is that at the same time they are also asking Congress and the FCC for more public airwaves—free of charge—so that they can provide new, improved and more profitable "digital" television.

Broadcasters also have argued in a pending U.S. Supreme Court case that cable systems should be forced to carry their signals at no cost.

But broadcasters cannot have it both ways. Either they accept the public interest obligations that go with the grant of free spectrum, or they should pay for the spectrum and any other special benefits they receive from competitors.

Some broadcasters argue that they already are providing three hours of children's educational and informational programming each week, and that some are doing more than that. So why are they fighting the FCC's proposal?

BROADCASTERS' OBJECTIONS

Broadcasters say that they don't want the government telling them what to do, but the truth is that while some broadcasters are indeed doing three hours, and a few are doing more, many are doing little or no children's educational and informational programming and they want to keep it that way.

We need a safety net for the bad broadcasters.

Others claim that "educational and informational programming" cannot be defined. But broadcasters know what is educational and informational. They know that the *Jetsons* is not. Or the *Flintstones*. Or *Scooby Doo*. Yet several years ago, a number of broadcasters told the FCC that these shows should count toward their children's television obligations.

As for the assertion that children don't watch educational television, the popularity of shows like *Sesame Street, Barney, Where in the World Is Carmen San Diego?* and *Bill Nye the Science Guy* prove that theory dead wrong.

THREE HOURS ISN'T TOO MUCH

To ask for three hours of [educational] programming a week isn't asking much. At least it would give families a few program choices. Equally important, under the FCC proposal, the definition of "educational" would be tightened and broadcasters would be required to label their shows. A private group may be appointed to comment on shows' quality. If so, broadcasters might not be so quick to call a program educational when it clearly isn't.

Christian Science Monitor, June 7, 1996.

The real problem is that many broadcasters show their educational programming before 7 a.m., when nobody is watching. And if children's educational programming gets lower ratings than entertainment programming, so what? There is no rule that says that broadcasters must make a huge profit on every show.

PUBLIC TRUSTEE OBLIGATIONS

Finally, the fact that cable provides some good kids' programming should not let commercial broadcasters off the hook. It is not enough to tell kids, "Let them eat cable."

Nearly one-third of Americans depend on over-the-air broadcasting as their sole video provider. And although public broadcasting does an excellent job of providing children's educational and informational programming, kids should not be forced to rely on it alone.

Children should have a choice of educational and informational programming from different sources. All broadcasters, not just public broadcasters, have free use of the public's spectrum, and therefore should be tasked with the same public trustee obligations.

| "Mandating three hours of
government-approved television
will not work."

REQUIRING MORE HOURS OF EDUCATIONAL TELEVISION WILL NOT BENEFIT CHILDREN

James Plummer

In the following viewpoint, James Plummer opposes a July 1996 agreement between the Federal Communications Commission (FCC) and television broadcasters that requires broadcasters to air three hours of educational programming a week. He contends that broadcasters will follow the letter of the agreement but will not produce good shows. Furthermore, according to Plummer, broadcasters are likely to demand free access to large portions of the broadcast spectrum in return for agreeing to the plan. Plummer is a policy analyst at Consumer Alert, a Washington-based free-market consumer group.

As you read, consider the following questions:
1. According to the author, who will decide what is and what is not educational under the new agreement?
2. What evidence does the author give that this plan will actually result in less choice of programming for parents?
3. According to Plummer, what will be the easiest way for broadcasters to respond to the new ruling?

Reprinted from James Plummer, "The Networks, Children's TV, and the Spectrum," *The Washington Times*, August 27, 1996, p. A19, by permission of *The Washington Times*.

The broadcast television industry has had another fit of social responsibility. After agreeing to a "voluntary" ratings system and offering free time for major presidential candidates, the broadcasters announced another act of alleged civic virtue on July 29, 1996. The broadcast industry has agreed to a plan requiring three hours of children's "educational" programming a week. These displays of public spirit on issues the television industry has supported for years conveniently come just as broadcasters argue for their God-given right to zillion-dollar spectrum space for digital television.

Now that the deal brokered between the White House and the National Association of Broadcasters has final approval by the Federal Communications Commission (FCC), some questions still linger about how the agreement will work. For instance: Who decides what is or is not "educational" television (disregarding the question of how educational any form of television can be)? In the final analysis, unelected bureaucrats at the FCC will decide what is good for your kids. What programs will meet your "child's intellectual/cognitive or social/emotional needs"? Some indication of what will be approved has already been given.

SAVED BY THE BELL

Greg Simon, the White House official who negotiated the plan, pointed to *Saved by the Bell* as an example. *Saved* follows the sitcom adventures of a group of high school students as they outwit their incompetent and fumbling principal and teachers week after week. Its routine "very special" episodes sermonize on everything from the virtue of the homeless to the ruthless greed of the oil company—which finds oil on campus and kills a few ducks that happen to be passing by. Few children over the age of seven take it seriously, but large numbers of postmodern preteens watch the show for camp value (in the 1990's, it seems even toddlers are innately postmodern), and to watch the cover-model kids.

Seated on the dais with the President at the dog and pony show announcing the agreement was liberal sweetheart Linda Ellerbee. Ms. Ellerbee hosts *Nick News*, a program on Nickelodeon and in syndication designed to drill the same liberal propaganda into the minds of children that adults get to see on the network news every night. Topics have run the gamut from Magic Johnson telling kids anyone can get AIDS to Rosie O'Donnell telling kids anyone can get big.

All this may be fine and good for some families that want their children to spout the conventional wisdom offered by the dominant liberal media. But under the new regime, parents will have less ability to decide what shows their kids watch, and the government will have more. One family may decide that the anti-business themes of *Captain Planet and the Planeteers* is not something their children should take to heart. The parents may feel television is better suited to teach the irony and cynicism imparted by Steven Spielberg's Warner Brothers cartoons. One of those shows, *Animaniacs!*, occasionally features the Wheel of Morality, a *Wheel of Fortune* type contraption which ridicules the "special message" portion of shows like *Planet*. Which do you think the FCC is more likely to approve as counting towards the three hours?

© Peter Steiner. Reprinted with permission.

The federal takeover comes as children's and educational programming is experiencing outstanding growth. Cable television, available to 98 percent of homes, and connected to 57 percent, provides a myriad of educational programming. Nickelodeon, [one of] America's leading cable channels, produces hours of quality, relatively intelligent, kids' entertainment (despite Ms. Ellerbee's shenanigans). Discovery and its sister station, The Learning Channel, have educational television more suitable for older children. And the state already has PBS to broadcast over the airwaves whatever shows it feels meet children's needs.

What does all of this mean for the average television viewing family? Some things are rather certain. The easiest way for a station to comply with the regulation is to air a regularly scheduled program that fits into the FCC's ephemeral definition of "educational." The networks have indicated they may produce such shows themselves for their affiliate stations to air. The new rules mandate the programming be shown between 7 a.m. and 10 p.m. The networks will have to devote about half an hour of valuable programming each day to pleasing Washington bureaucrats instead of the viewing public. Even in the era of cable and satellites, it is still the broadcast networks that have the most resources and widest reach. As more and more viewers turn away from broadcast television, hampered by new regulations, it will be impossible to know what exactly the viewing public has lost.

PLAYING A TRUMP CARD

Yet the networks know that they have lost something, and they aren't shy about demanding something in return. Can anyone not see the networks using their "public service" as a trump card in the debate over spectrum rights? As communications services and technology expand, large portions of the broadcast spectrum, which the FCC regulates, are in high demand. The broadcast industry wants a large chunk of spectrum to broadcast programming digitally. Digital broadcasts are of higher audio-visual quality and take up more spectrum than today's analog standards. What the spectrum broadcasters are angling for is worth up to $100 billion.

The FCC could auction off the spectrum, which could be used for any number of services: cellular phones, satellite television, high-speed wireless Internet access, even CD-quality radio. An open auction of spectrum would lead to countless innovations in the communications industry, no doubt including a host of services geared to meet the needs of American families.

The FCC should encourage innovation in programming by unleashing the market to respond to the informational needs of children and their families. Mandating three hours of government-approved television will not work. And a quid pro quo exchange of free speech for spectrum property rights will do untold and unseen damage to the future of communication.

PERIODICAL BIBLIOGRAPHY

The following articles have been selected to supplement the diverse views presented in this chapter. Addresses are provided for periodicals not indexed in the *Readers' Guide to Periodical Literature*, the *Alternative Press Index*, the *Social Sciences Index*, or the *Index to Legal Periodicals and Books*.

Joe Chidley	"Toxic TV," *Maclean's*, June 17, 1996.
John Davidson	"Menace to Society: Worried About Media Violence? Cartoons May Be the Real Culprit," *Rolling Stone*, February 22, 1996.
Barbara Dority and John Perry Barlow	"Ratings and the V-Chip," *Humanist*, May/June 1996.
Jib Fowles	"The Violence Against Television Violence," *Television Quarterly*, Winter 1996.
Max Frankel	"Live at 11: Death," *New York Times Magazine*, June 15, 1997.
Malcolm Gladwell	"Chip Thrills: There's More to TV than V. There's Also T," *New Yorker*, January 20, 1997.
Matthew Hogben	"Factors Moderating the Effect of Televised Aggression on Viewer Behavior," *Communication Research*, April 1998.
Kenneth Jost	"Children's Television: Will the New Regulations Make It Better?" *CQ Researcher*, August 15, 1997. Available from 1414 22nd St. NW, Washington, DC 20037.
Jay Kist	"Does TV Affect Your Psyche?" *Current Health*, December 2, 1996.
Greg Makris	"The Myth of a Technological Solution to Television Violence: Identifying Problems with the V-Chip," *Journal of Communication Inquiry*, Fall 1996. Available from Iowa Center for Communication Study, University of Iowa, School of Journalism and Mass Communication, Iowa City, IA 52242.
Anu Mustonen and Lea Pulkkinen	"Television Violence: A Development of a Coding Scheme," *Journal of Broadcasting & Electronic Media*, Spring 1997.

Steve Perron   "Hard Decisions for TV News," *St. Louis
                      Journalism Review*, September 1997. Available
                      from 470 E. Lockwood, Suite 414, St. Louis,
                      MO 63119-3914.

John P. Sisk   "The Poetry of Violence," *American Scholar*,
                      Spring 1997.

Christopher Stern   "Researchers Shocked to Find—TV Violence,"
                      Variety, April 20, 1998. Available from 249 W.
                      17th St., New York, NY 10011.

Matthew Stevenson   "America Unplugged," *American Enterprise*,
                      September/October 1997.

Allan S. Vann   "Kids, Media, and Family Values," *Education
                      Digest*, March 1996.

FOR FURTHER DISCUSSION

CHAPTER 1

1. Kevin W. Saunders and Kevin Durkin describe a number of experimental methods used to determine whether television violence causes violence in children. What seem to be the best methods for studying the causal relationship between television and violence? Why? What are the limitations of these methods? Based on your reading of these viewpoints, do you believe television violence causes violent behavior in children? Why or why not?

2. Both Joe McNamara and Jeff Greenfield agree that America has experienced significant cultural change since World War II, although they attribute the change to different causes. According to their viewpoints, in what ways has American culture changed since 1945? Do you believe this change represents a decline in values? Why or why not? To what extent is television responsible for these changes? Defend your answers by citing the viewpoints.

CHAPTER 2

1. Raymond A. Schroth contends that advertising is an inherently deceitful and damaging enterprise. John E. Calfee argues that advertising plays a positive role in a democratic society. Whose argument is more persuasive? Why?

2. Do you think that banning tobacco ads would help prevent children and teens from buying tobacco products? Why or why not? Would a ban on tobacco ads undermine free speech? Defend your answers with references to the viewpoints by Jack Reed and John Berlau.

CHAPTER 3

1. The first two viewpoints of this chapter address the issues of media bias. What kinds of evidence do the authors use to argue for and against the existence of such bias? Whose use of evidence is most convincing? Why? Based on your reading of these viewpoints, do you think that most journalists are conservative, liberal, or middle-of-the-road? Use at least two examples from the viewpoints to support your conclusion.

2. Briefly summarize the arguments for and against the use of opinion polls in politics as expressed by Robert Kubey, Vincent M. Fitzgerald, Godfrey Sperling, and Andrew Kohut. Whose argument(s) do you find most effective and why?

3. President Bill Clinton argues that providing free airtime for political candidates will help keep elections focused on the issues rather than on fund-raising. Edward O. Fritts, however, believes that candidates already receive considerable free airtime and do not use all the time available to them now. Having read both viewpoints, do you think that providing free airtime to candidates would help the democratic process? Why or why not?

CHAPTER 4

1. William F. Buckley Jr. argues that the Supreme Court should not have ruled the Communications Decency Act (CDA) unconstitutional. Are his reasons for this stance valid? Why or why not? What evidence does Brock N. Meeks provide to support his contention that the CDA would harm free speech on the Internet? Do you find his argument convincing? Why or why not?

2. The American Library Association argues that filtering pornographic sites in libraries will be ineffective and will undermine the free speech of library users. David Burt, however, argues that filtering is an effective way of assuring that children do not access inappropriate sites on the Internet in libraries. Whose argument is most compelling? Why?

3. All blocking software requires some kind of rating system so that appropriate sites may be blocked out. C. Dianne Martin and Joseph M. Reagle Jr. argue that the best plan is to have Internet sites rate themselves. Nadine Strossen believes that even self-rating will harm free speech. What evidence do the authors of these two viewpoints provide for the effectiveness of self-rating systems? Do you believe that self-rating violates free speech? Why or why not?

CHAPTER 5

1. Both Gloria Tristani and Bob Gale write about the effectiveness of the V-chip from vested points of view. Tristani is commissioner of the Federal Communications Commission and Gale is a Hollywood movie producer. How might their occupations influence their views on the V-chip? What position do you find most convincing? Why?

2. All monitoring technology, like the V-chip, depends on rating systems through which inappropriate programs can be blocked. Jack Valenti believes this can best be accomplished by an age-based, rather than content-based, system. What arguments does he use to support this position? Is he persuasive? Why or why

not? Frank Rich argues that ratings will not work because they will not change Americans' viewing habits. Do you find this argument convincing? Why or why not?

3. Gigi B. Sohn believes that broadcasters should be required to air additional hours of educational television in order to improve the quality and quantity of children's programming. However, James Plummer argues that such a requirement will have many unintended consequences. Which viewpoint makes the better case for improving children's programming? Why?

GENERAL QUESTIONS

1. Many of the issues discussed in this book pit a concern for public values, like wholesome entertainment, against a concern for the First Amendment value of free speech. How important is free speech to a democratic society? How far should it be tolerated? Should a pornographic Internet site be blocked if it means that other, nonpornographic sites might also be blocked? Explain your answer.

2. To what extent are the modern media responsible for shaping public and personal values? Do you believe that the media should be monitored and restricted to reflect appropriate values or do you believe the media should be relatively unrestricted? Various means of restricting media content are discussed in the viewpoints presented in this book. In your opinion, what is the best way to monitor the media and control their portrayals of sex and violence?

ORGANIZATIONS TO CONTACT

The editors have compiled the following list of organizations concerned with issues debated in this book. The descriptions are derived from materials provided by the organizations. All have publications or information available for interested readers. The list was compiled on the date of publication of the present volume; the information provided here may change. Be aware that many organizations take several weeks or longer to respond to inquiries, so allow as much time as possible.

American Advertising Federation (AAF)
1101 Vermont Ave. NW, Suite 500, Washington, DC 20005-6306
(202) 898-0089 • fax: (202) 898-0159
e-mail: aaf@aaf.org • website: http://www.aaf.org

AAF is a professional advertising association representing corporate advertisers, agencies, media companies, suppliers, and academia. The organization protects and promotes the well-being of advertising. It publishes the quarterly *American Advertising*.

American Civil Liberties Union (ACLU)
132 W. 43rd St., New York, NY 10036
(212) 944-9800
website: http://www.aclu.org

The ACLU champions the rights set forth in the Declaration of Independence and the Constitution, and it opposes censoring any form of speech. The ACLU publishes the quarterly newsletter *Civil Liberties Alert* and several handbooks, public policy reports, project reports, civil liberties books, and pamphlets, including one on the Freedom of Information Act. It also has a "Materials and Resources" web page for students.

American Library Association (ALA)
50 E. Huron, Chicago, IL 60611
(800) 545-2433 • fax: (312) 440-9374
e-mail: ala@ala.org • website: http://www.ala.org

ALA is the oldest and largest library association in the world. It works to protect intellectual freedom and to promote high-quality library and information services. ALA publishes the *Newsletter on Intellectual Freedom*, pamphlets, articles, posters, and an annually updated *Banned Books Week Resource Kit*.

Center for Investigative Reporting (CIR)
500 Howard St., Suite 206, San Francisco, CA 94105-3000
(415) 543-1200 • fax: (415) 543-8311
e-mail: cir@igc.org • website: http://www.muckraker.org

CIR is a nonprofit news organization composed of journalists dedicated to encouraging investigative reporting. It conducts investigations, offers consulting services to news and special-interest organizations, and conducts workshops and seminars for investigative journalists. Its publications include the seasonal magazine *Muckraker* and the *Investigative Handbook*.

Fairness and Accuracy in Reporting (FAIR)
130 W. 25th St., New York, NY 10001
(212) 633-6700 • fax: (212) 727-7668
e-mail: fair@fair.org • website: http://www.fair.org
FAIR is a national media watchdog group that offers documented criticism of media bias and censorship. It believes that the media are controlled by, and support, corporate and governmental interests and that they are insensitive to women, labor, minorities, and other special-interest groups. It publishes the bimonthly magazine *Extra!*

Freedom Forum Media Studies Center
580 Madison Ave., New York, NY 10022
(212) 317-6500
e-mail: mfitzsi@mediastudies.org
website: http://www.freedomforum.org
The center is a research organization dedicated to studying the media and educating the public about their influence on society. It publishes numerous conference reports and papers, including *The Media and Women* and the biannual *Media Studies Journal*.

Media Institute
1000 Potomac St. NW, Suite 301, Washington, DC 20007
(202) 298-7512 • fax: (202) 337-7092
e-mail: tmi@clark.net • website: http://www.mediainst.org
The Media Institute is a nonprofit research foundation that specializes in communications-policy issues. It exists to foster three goals: freedom of speech, deregulation of the media and communications industry, and excellence in journalism. Its publications include *The First Amendment and the Media* and *Unreasonable Access: Another Turn of the Regulatory Spin Cycle*.

Media Research Center (MRC)
113 S. West St., 2nd Fl., Alexandria, VA 22314
(703) 683-9733
e-mail: mrc@mediaresearch.org • website: http://www.mrc.org
The center is a conservative media watchdog organization concerned with what it perceives to be a liberal bias in the news and entertainment media. In 1995 it opened the Parents Television Council to bring family programming back to television. MRC publishes the monthly newsletters *Media Watch* and *Notable Quotables*.

Morality in the Media (MIM)
475 Riverside Dr., Suite 239, New York, NY 10115
(212) 870-3222 • fax: (212) 870-2765
e-mail: mimnyc@ix.netcom.com
website: http://pw2.netcom.com

Established in 1962, MIM is a national, not-for-profit interfaith organization that works to combat obscenity and to uphold decency standards in the media. It maintains the National Obscenity Law Center, a clearinghouse of legal materials, and conducts public information programs to involve concerned citizens. It publishes the *Morality in Media Newsletter* and the handbook *TV: The World's Greatest Mind-Bender*.

National Association of Black Journalists

8701A Adelphi Rd., Adelphi, MD 20783-1716
(301) 445-7100 • fax: (301) 445-7101
e-mail: nabj@nabj.org • website: http://www.nabj.org

Founded in 1975, the National Association of Black Journalists serves to strengthen ties among African American journalists, promote diversity in newsrooms, and honor the achievements of black journalists. It publishes the *NABJ Journal* ten times a year.

National Coalition Against Censorship

275 Seventh Ave., New York, NY 10001
(212) 807-6222 • fax: (212) 807-6245
e-mail: ncac@ncac.org • website: http://www.ncac.org

The coalition opposes censorship in any form, believing it to be against the First Amendment right to freedom of speech. It works to educate the public about the dangers of censorship, including censorship of violence on television and in movies and music. The coalition publishes *Censorship News* five times a year and reports such as *The Sex Panic: Women, Censorship, and "Pornography."*

National Coalition on Television Violence

33290 W. 14 Mile Rd., Suite 498, West Bloomfield, MI 48322
(810) 489-3177
e-mail: reach@nctvv.org • website: http://www.nctvv.org

The coalition is an educational and research organization committed to decreasing the amount of violence on television and in films. It sponsors speakers and seminars and publishes ratings and reviews of films and television programs. The coalition produces reports, educational materials, and the *NCTV Journal*.

National Council of Teachers of English (NCTE)

1111 W. Kenyon Rd., Urbana, IL 61801-1096
(217) 328-3870 • fax: (217) 328-9645
website: http://www.ncte.org

NCTE is an alliance of organizations committed to defending freedom of thought, inquiry, and expression by engaging in public education advocacy on national and local levels. It believes that censorship of violent materials is dangerous because it represses intellectual and artistic freedom. Its publications include the *Quarterly Review of Doublespeak*.

Parents Television Council (PTC)

7905 Hollywood Blvd., #1010, Hollywood, CA 90028
(213) 621-2506
website: http://www.parentstv.org

PTC was founded in 1995 as the Hollywood project of the Media Research Center. It publishes special reports focusing on a variety of topics relating to the content of prime-time television—including in-depth analyses of the family hour and the new television rating system. It publishes *The Family Guide to Prime Time Television*.

Society for the Eradication of Television (SET)

Box 10491, Oakland, CA 94610-0491
(510) 763-8712

SET members oppose television and encourage others to stop all television viewing. The society believes television "retards the inner life of human beings, destroys human interaction, and squanders time." SET maintains a speakers bureau and reference library and publishes manuals and pamphlets, the periodic *Propaganda War* Comix, and the quarterly *SET Free: The Newsletter Against Television*.

BIBLIOGRAPHY OF BOOKS

Akhil Reed Amar
and Alan Hirsch

For the People: What the Constitution Really Says About Your Rights. New York: Free Press, 1998.

Stephen Ansolabehere
and Shanto Iyengar

Going Negative: How Political Advertisements Shrink and Polarize the Electorate. New York: Free Press, 1996.

E.M. Barendt, ed.

Libel Law and the Media: The Chilling Effect. New York: Clarendon Press, 1996.

Ralph D. Barney
and Jay Black, eds.

Exploring Questions of Media Morality. Mahwah, NJ: Lawrence Erlbaum, 1996.

Arthur Charity

Doing Public Journalism. New York: Guilford Press, 1995.

Elizabeth C. Childs

Suspended License: Censorship and the Visual Arts. Seattle: University of Washington Press, 1998.

J.M. Coetzee

Giving Offense: Essays on Censorship. Chicago: University of Chicago Press, 1996.

Jeff Cohen and
Norman Solomon

Adventures in Medialand: Behind the News, Beyond the Pundits. Monroe, ME: Common Courage Press, 1995.

Jeff Cohen and
Norman Solomon

Through the Media Looking Glass: Decoding Bias and Blather in the News. Monroe, ME: Common Courage Press, 1995.

David Croteau
and William Hoynes

By Invitation Only: How the Media Limits Political Debate. Monroe, ME: Common Courage Press, 1995.

Judith Wagner Decew

In Pursuit of Privacy: Law, Ethics, and the Rise of Technology. Ithaca, NY: Cornell University Press, 1997.

Edwin Diamond and
Robert A. Silverman

White House to Your House: Media and Politics in Virtual America. Cambridge, MA: MIT Press, 1995.

C. Thomas Dienes et al.

Newsgathering and the Law. Charlottesville, VA: Michie Press, 1997.

Ralph Engelman

Public Radio and Television in America. Thousand Oaks, CA: Sage, 1996.

James Fallows

Breaking the News: How the Media Undermine American Democracy. New York: Pantheon Books, 1996.

Martha A. Fineman and
Martha T. McCluskey

Feminism, Media, and the Law. New York: Oxford University Press, 1997.

James S. Fishkin

Media Power in Politics. 3rd ed. Washington, DC: Congressional Quarterly Books, 1996.

James S. Fishkin

The Voice of the People: Public Opinion and Democracy. New Haven, CT: Yale University Press, 1995.

Laura Flanders	*Real Majority, Media Minority: The Costs of Sidelining Women in Reporting.* Monroe, ME: Common Courage Press, 1997.
David French and Michael Richards, eds.	*Contemporary Television—Eastern Perspectives.* Thousand Oaks, CA: Sage, 1996.
Jack Fuller	*News Values: Ideas for an Information Age.* Chicago: University of Chicago Press, 1996.
John H. Garvey and Frederick F. Schauer	*The First Amendment: A Reader.* St. Paul: West, 1996.
George Gerbner, Hamid Mowlana, and Herbert I. Schiller, eds.	*Invisible Crises: What Conglomerate Control of Media Means for America and the World.* Boulder, CO: Westview Press, 1996.
James C. Goodale	*Communications Law.* New York: Practicing Law Institute, 1996.
Doris A. Graber	*Mass Media and American Politics.* 5th ed. Washington, DC: Congressional Quarterly Books, 1996.
Louis E. Ingelhart	*Press and Speech Freedoms in America, 1619–1995: A Chronology.* Westport, CT: Greenwood, 1997.
Phyllis Kaniss	*The Media and the Mayor's Race: The Failure of Urban Political Reporting.* Bloomington: Indiana University Press, 1995.
Richard T. Kaplar, ed.	*The First Amendment and the Media, 1997: An Assessment of Free Speech and a Free Press.* Washington, DC: Media Institute, 1997.
Richard T. Kaplar and Patrick D. Maines	*The Government Factor: Undermining Journalistic Ethics in the Information Age.* Washington, DC: Cato Institute, 1995.
John Leonard	*Smoke and Mirrors: Violence, Television, and Other American Cultures.* New York: New Press, 1997.
Newton N. Minow and Craig L. Lamay	*Abandoned in the Wasteland: Children, Television, and the First Amendment.* New York: Hill and Wang, 1995.
Brigitte Nacos	*Terrorism and the Media: From the Iran Hostage Crisis to the Oklahoma City Bombing.* New York: Columbia University Press, 1996.
Marvin Olasky	*Telling the Truth: How to Revitalize Christian Journalism.* Wheaton, IL: Crossway Press, 1996.
Benjamin I. Page	*Who Deliberates? Mass Media in Modern Democracy.* Chicago: University of Chicago Press, 1996.
Monroe E. Price	*Television, the Public Sphere, and National Identity.* Oxford: Clarendon, 1996.

John P. Robinson and Geoffrey Godbey	*Time for Life: The Surprising Ways Americans Use Their Time.* University Park: Pennsylvania State University Press, 1997.
Kevin W. Saunders	*Violence as Obscenity: Limiting the Media's First Amendment Protection.* Durham, NC: Duke University Press, 1996.
Danny Schechter	*The More You Watch the Less You Know.* Edison, NJ: Seven Stories Press, 1998.
Herbert I. Schiller	*Information Inequality: The Deepening Social Crisis in America.* New York: Routledge, 1996.
Martin Shaw	*Civil Society and Media in Global Crises: Representing Distant Violence.* London: Pinter, 1997.
John Sinclair, Stuart Cunningham, and Elizabeth Jack, eds.	*New Patterns in Global Television—Peripheral Vision.* Oxford: Oxford University Press, 1996.
Norman Solomon and Jeff Cohen	*Wizards of Media Oz: Behind the Curtain of Mainstream News.* Monroe, ME: Common Courage Press, 1997.
Steven D. Stark	*Glued to the Set: The Sixty Television Shows and Events That Made Us Who We Are Today.* New York: Free Press, 1997.
Lance Strate, Ronald Jacobson, and Stephanie B. Gibson, eds.	*Communication and Cyberspace: Social Interaction in an Electronic Environment.* Cresskill, NJ: Hampton Press, 1996.
Roger Streitmatter	*Mightier than the Sword: How the News Media Have Shaped American History.* Boulder, CO: Westview Press, 1997.
George W.S. Trow	*Within the Context of No Context.* New York: Atlantic Monthly Press, 1997.
Joseph Turow	*Breaking Up America: Advertisers and the New Media World.* Chicago: University of Chicago Press, 1997.
James B. Twitchell	*Adcult USA: The Triumph of Advertising in American Culture.* New York: Columbia University Press, 1995.

INDEX